MACMILLAN
MUSIC and YOU

Cover Design and Illustration
Heather Cooper

Illustration Credits
Marilyn Bass
Alex Bloch
Alan Eitzen
Simon Galkin
Richard Hooks
Robert Jackson
Ron Lehew
Richard Loehle
Robert Lo Grippo
Verlin Miller
Isidre Mones
Hima Pamoedjo
Jan Pyk
Lee Sievers
Fred Winkowski

MACMILLAN
MUSIC and YOU

Barbara Staton
Merrill Staton
Marilyn Davidson
Nancy Ferguson

Macmillan Publishing Company

New York

Collier Macmillan Publishers

London

ACKNOWLEDGMENTS

Grateful acknowledgment is given to the following authors and publishers. In the case of songs and poems for which acknowledgment is not given, we have earnestly endeavored to find the original source and to procure permission for their use, but without success. Extensive research failed to locate the author and/or copyright holder.

Aldi Music Co./Ireneadele Music Pub. Co. for *On the Sunny Side of the Street* by Jimmy McHugh and Dorothy Fields, arranged by Hawley Ades. Copyright © 1930 Aldi Music Company and Ireneadele Publishing Company pursuant to sections 304(c) and 40(b) of the U.S. Copyright Law.

Shalom Altman for *Vine and Fig Tree*, music by Shalom Altman. Hebrew words from Isaiah. Words and melody copyright © 1948 by Shalom Altman. Used by permission of his Estate. English verson by Leah Jaffe and Fran Minkoff.

Hank Beebe for the musical *Pioneering*. Copyright © 1985 by Hank Beebe. All rights reserved.

Belwin-Mills Publishing Corp. for *Carol from an Irish Cabin* by Dale Wood. Copyright © 1970 by Schmitt Music Center. Reprinted by permission of Belwin-Mills Publishing Corp. All rights reserved; *The Girl I Left Behind Me* by Leroy Anderson from THE IRISH SUITE. Copyright © 1950 by Mills Music, Inc. Copyright renewed. Used by permission. All rights reserved.

Kay C. Bennett for *Loneliness Song* (Shi-Naa-Sha). Reprinted by courtesy of Kay C. Bennett.

Kenneth C. Bennett for *A Modern Dragon* by Rowena Bastin Bennett. Reprinted by permission of Kenneth C. Bennett.

Cherry Lane Music Publishing Company for *Thank God I'm a Country Boy* by John Martin Sommers. Copyright © 1974 Cherry Lane Music Publishing Co., Inc. All rights reserved. Used by permission.

Columbia Pictures Publications for *Tomorrow* and *It's the Hard-Knock Life* by C. Strouse/M. Charnin. Copyright © 1977 by Charles Strouse and Edwin H. Morris & Co., a division of MPL Communications, Inc. All Rights of CHARLES STROUSE Administered by SONGWRITERS GUILD, 276 5th Ave., New York, NY 10019, I-M-A; *Tiger Rag* by the Original Dixieland Jazz Band. Copyright © 1917 (renewed 1945) Leo Feist, Inc. All rights of Leo Feist, Inc. Assigned to CBS Catalogue Partnership. All rights controlled and administered by CBS Feist Catalog I-M-A.

Marilyn Davidson for *Winter Thunderstorm Chant—Ice and Sleet*. Reprinted by permission of the author, Marilyn Davidson.

Judith Eisenstein for *O Hanukah* from GATEWAY TO JEWISH SONG. Reprinted by permission of Judith Eisenstein.

Carl Fischer, Inc. for *Winter Song* by Stephen Paulus. Copyright © 1976 by Carl Fischer, Inc., New York. International Copyright Secured. All rights reserved. Reprinted by permission; *Isn't It Reassuring*, two-part chorus with piano and percussion by Natalie Sleeth. Copyright © 1973 by Carl Fischer, Inc., New York. All rights reserved. Used by permission.

Geordie Music Publishing Company for *Skin and Bones* by Jean Ritchie. Copyright © 1952 Jean Ritchie. Geordie Music Publishing Co.

Hampton University for *Sun Don't Set in the Mornin'*, a southern Folk Hymn from RELIGIOUS FOLK SONGS OF THE NEGRO by R. Nathaniel Dett, 1927. Reprinted courtesy of Hampton University Archives, Hampton, VA.

Harcourt Brace Jovanovich, Inc. for *Some Opposites* from OPPOSITES by Richard Wilbur. Copyright © 1973 by Richard Wilbur. Reprinted by permission of Harcourt Brace Jovanovich, Inc.; *Buffalo Dusk* from SMOKE AND STEEL by Carl Sandburg. Copyright © 1920 by Harcourt Brace Jovanovich, Inc., renewed 1948 by Carl Sandburg. Reprinted by permission of the publisher.

Hinshaw Music, Inc. for *Winter's a Drag Rag* by Natalie Sleeth from WEEKDAY SONGBOOK. Copyright © 1977 by Hinshaw Music, Inc. Reprinted by permission.

Instructor Magazine for *Boogie Woogie Ghost* by Nadine L. Pelgar. Reprinted from INSTRUCTOR, October 1973. Copyright © 1973 by the Instructor Publications, Inc. Used by permission.

Jan-Lee Music, Inc. for *Let There Be Peace on Earth* by Sy Miller and Jill Jackson. Copyright © 1955 by Jan-Lee Music. Copyright renewed 1983. Used by permission.

Jobete Music Company, Inc. for *Reach Out and Touch*, Words and Music by Nickolas Ashford and Valerie Simpson. Copyright © 1970 Jobete Music Co., Inc. Used by permission. International Copyright Secured. All rights reserved.

Laura Koulish for *The Breath of Winter*. Copyright © 1985 by Laura Koulish. Reprinted by permission of the author.

Hal Leonard Corporation for *Peanut Vendor*, English words by Marion Sunshine and L. Wolfe Gilbert. Music and Spanish words by Moises Simons. Copyright © 1928, 1929, 1932 by Edward B. Marks Music Company. Copyright renewed. International Copyright Secured. All rights reserved. Used by permission.

Macmillan Publishing Company
866 Third Avenue
New York, N.Y. 10022
Collier Macmillan Canada, Inc.

Printed in the United States of America

ISBN: 0-02-293390-5
9 8 7 6 5 4 3 2 1

AUTHORS

Barbara Staton holds a B.S. degree in Music Education and an M.A. in Dance and Related Arts. She has taught music at all levels, elementary through college, and has served as a television teacher in Georgia. She is the author of a four-volume series of books and records designed to teach music concepts through movement. Ms. Staton has written numerous songs for television and recordings and is a composer member of ASCAP. She now resides in Alpine, New Jersey, writing and testing educational materials.

Dr. Merrill Staton is nationally known as a music educator, choral director, singer, composer, and record producer. He has been music director of and has conducted the Merrill Staton Voices on many network TV series and recordings. He has been a leader in the field of music education for the past twenty-five years. Dr. Staton pioneered the use of children's voices on recordings for education. He earned his M.A. and Ed.D. degrees from Teachers College, Columbia University.

Marilyn Davidson teaches elementary general music in Pequannock, New Jersey. She also teaches graduate summer courses in music education at Potsdam University of New York; the Hartt School of Music at the University of Hartford in West Hartford, Connecticut; and Teachers College, Columbia University, in New York City. Her teaching experience spans twenty-eight years at all levels.

Nancy Ferguson holds a Master of Arts degree from Memphis State University, a B.S. degree in Music Education from Murray State University, and an Orff Teacher's Certificate from the Royal Conservatory of Music in Toronto. Ms. Ferguson has published a number of articles and books on music. Currently, she is the Elementary Music Supervisor for the Memphis city schools, Memphis, Tennessee.

SPECIAL CONTRIBUTORS

Dr. Betty Atterbury — Mainstreaming ● **Marshia Beck** — Movement ● **Mary Frances Early** — Black American Music ● **Joan Gregoryk** — Vocal Development

● **Dr. Janos Horvath** — Kodály ● **Virginia Mead** — Dalcroze ● **Mollie Tower** — Listening Selections ◀

CONSULTANTS AND CONTRIBUTING WRITERS

Dr. Betty Atterbury, University of Southern Maine, Gorham, Maine ● **Marshia Beck,** Holy Names College, Oakland, California ● **Diane Bennette,** Bergenfield Public Schools, Bergenfield, New Jersey ● **Teri Burdett,** Barnsley Elementary, Rockville, Maryland ● **Dr. Robert A. Duke,** University of Texas, Austin, Texas ● **Mary Frances Early,** Atlanta Public Schools, Atlanta, Georgia ● **Nancy Ferguson,** Memphis Public Schools, Memphis, Tennessee ● **Diane Fogler,** Rockaway Township Public Schools, Rockaway, New Jersey ● **Joan Gregoryk,** Chevy Chase Elementary, Chevy Chase, Maryland ● **Dr. Janos Horvath,** University of Calgary, Calgary, Alberta, Canada ● **Dr. Judith A. Jellison,** University of Texas, Austin, Texas ● **Dr. JaFran Jones,** Bowling Green State University, Bowling Green, Ohio ● **James Kenward,** Howe Avenue Elementary, Sacramento, California ● **Tom Kosmala,** Pittsburgh Public Schools, Pittsburgh, Pennsylvania ● **Virginia Mead,** Kent State University, Kent, Ohio ● **Belle San Miguel-Ortiz,** San Antonio Independent School District, San Antonio, Texas ● **Jane Pippart,** Lancaster Public Schools, Lancaster, Pennsylvania ● **Dr. Susan Snyder,** Hamilton Avenue Elementary, Greenwich, Connecticut ● **Mollie Tower,** Austin Independent School District, Austin, Texas

contents

unit 1

An American Music Sampler *1*

The American Beat Goes On 2
Finding the Strong Beat 4
Fife and Drum 8
Theme and Variations 10
Working to the Tempo 12
Another Kind of Chantey 16
A Working Rhythm 18
A Song of the Shakers 20
A Famous Theme and Variations 22
An Early Dance Tune 24
Take Another Look 26
Just Checking 27

unit 2

Singing America at Work and Play *28*

Songs for Work and Play 30
Tonal Center 33
Work Songs of the Railroad 36
Express Yourself! 40
Ghostly Rhythm Patterns 42
Singing with Expression 46
Take Another Look 48
Just Checking 49

unit 3

The American Beat Moves West! *50*

Moving in Tempo 52
Listening for Loud and Soft 56
Move to the Strong Beat 60
Native American Arts 64
The Beat in $\frac{4}{4}$ Meter 66
A Thanksgiving Round 68
Take Another Look 70
Just Checking 71

unit 4

The Winter Holiday Beat 72

Syncopation: An Exciting Rhythm! 74
Major and Minor 78
Identifying and Writing Syncopated Patterns 82
Songs in Major and Minor 86
Dynamic Markings 88
Holiday Partners 92
Take Another Look 94
Just Checking 95
Related Arts:
Billy the Kid 96

unit 5

Sounds and Textures 100

The Percussion Family 102
Music Texture: Thick and Thin 108
A Percussion Accompaniment 110
Creating Different Textures 112
Rondo Form 114
Create a Winter Rondo 118
Weaving Rhythms and Harmony 120
Rhythm Patterns in a Creole Song 124
Listening for Different Meters 127
Singing a Song in $\frac{3}{4}$ Meter 128
Take Another Look 130
Just Checking 131
Related Arts:
Callin' the Dog 132

unit 6

American Music on Parade 142

A Song from Long Ago 144
Band or Orchestra? 150
A Favorite Song of Abraham Lincoln 156
A Musical Map 160
A Rhythmic Tongue Twister 162
Form in American Marches 167
Take Another Look 168
Just Checking 169

unit 7

Twentieth Century American Beat 170

The Roots of Jazz 172
An Old Song in a New Style 174
The Sound of Dixieland Bands 176
A New Rhythm Pattern 180
Musical Interlude 182
A Song That's Just for Fun 184
Jazz and "Swing" 186
Singing with Rhythm 190
Playing the Bells 192
Folk Percussion Instruments 193
Take Another Look 194
Just Checking 195

unit 8

The American Beat Goes On 196

Symphony Orchestras 198
Meter Signature 206
West Side Story 210
Listening for Meter 211
Sounds of the Sixties 212
Flats and Sharps 216
A Broadway Musical of the 1970s 220
Variations in Dynamic Levels 224
New Music 226
A Grand Finale 230
Take Another Look 232
Just Checking 233
Focus on:
Charles Strouse 234
Musical:
Pioneering 236

Songbook 245

More Choral Music 284

Playing the Recorder 297

Glossary of Terms 301
Classified Index 304
Listening Selections 306
Alphabetical Song Index 307

UNIT **1**

AN AMERICAN MUSIC SAMPLER

The American beat and
the American spirit—
past and present—
are carried on
through music.

 "American Music Montage"

• Pat the beat. Listen for the changes in tempo.

1

THE AMERICAN BEAT GOES ON

Songs by Woody Guthrie showed his love and concern for the people and places of the United States.

This Land Is Your Land

Words and music by Woody Guthrie

This land is your land,____ This land is my land____ ____ from Cal - i - for - nia ____ to the New York is - land,____

D. C. (*da capo*) means you go back to the beginning. **Al fine** means to sing or play until you reach the word *fine*. **Fine** means the end.

FINDING THE STRONG BEAT

"Yankee Doodle" is a favorite song from the time of the American Revolution.

● Listen for the steady marching beat of the drum.

The Yankee Doodle, a mural painted by Norman Rockwell

Yankee Doodle

Traditional
Words by Dr. Richard Shuckburgh

1. Fath'r and I went down to camp
2. Yan - kee Doo - dle went to town,

a - long with Cap - tain Good - in',
a - rid - ing on a po - ny,

and there we saw the men and boys
He stuck a feath - er in his cap

as thick as hast - y pud - din'.
and called it mac - a - ron - i.

NG ON A PONY · STUCK A FEATHER IN HIS HAT · AND CALLED IT MACARONI

Yankee Doodle, Norman Rockwell, courtesy NASSAU INN, Princeton, NJ.

Refrain

Yan - kee Doo - dle keep it up, Yan - kee Doo - dle dan - dy,

Mind the mu - sic and the step, and with the girls be han - dy.

3. There was Captain Washington
   Upon a slapping stallion,
   A-giving orders to his men;
   I guess there were a million.

4. And there I saw a swamping gun,
   Large as a log of maple,
   Upon a mighty little cart;
   A load for Father's cattle.

5. And every time they fired it off,
   It took a horn of powder;
   It made a noise like Father's gun
   Only a nation louder.

6. And there I saw a little keg,
   Its head all made of leather,
   They knocked upon't with little sticks
   To call the folks together.

7. I can't tell you half I saw,
   They kept up such a smother;
   I took my hat off, made a bow,
   And scampered home to Mother.

5

A **beat** is a unit of time.

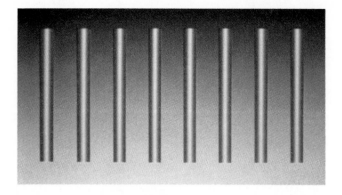

● Clap each beat.

Beats may be grouped into combinations of stronger and weaker beats like this:

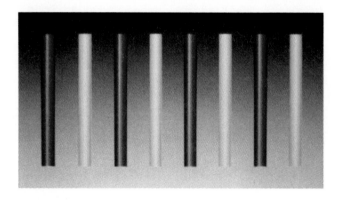

● Pat the strong beat. Clap the weak beat.

The strong beat is the first beat after the bar line.

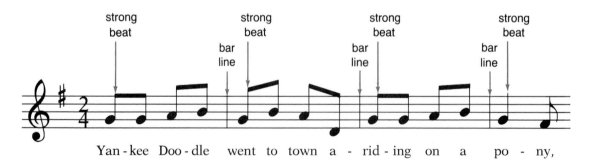

Yan - kee Doo - dle   went to town a - rid - ing on a   po - ny,

● Sing the second verse of "Yankee Doodle" again. Pat and clap the beat as you sing. Be sure to pat on the strong beat.

You have clapped and patted the beat and strong beat in "Yankee Doodle."

- Clap the rhythm of the melody for the second verse of "Yankee Doodle."

Three of the sounds are one beat long. They are called **quarter notes** and look like this ♩.

The other sounds are shorter. They are called **eighth notes** and stand for two equal sounds to one beat. They look like this ♫.

- Find the eighth and quarter notes in the verse of "Yankee Doodle."

FIFE AND DRUM

This famous picture portrays the revolutionary spirit of American independence. It shows music's part in expressing this spirit.

The Spirit of '76 is a famous patriotic scene painted by Archibald M. Willard. It shows a fife player and two drummers leading American troops during the Revolutionary War.

A fife is a small, high-pitched woodwind, similar to a flute. It is often used in military bands or played with drums in a fife and drum corps (côr). Fife and drum players often led soldiers into battle during the American Revolution. The fife and drum corps also helped create a patriotic spirit among soldiers and civilians.

"The Girl I Left Behind Me" is a soldier's song that was popular in 1776.

● Listen to the song played by a fife and drum corps.

 "The Girl I Left Behind Me"

● Listen again. Raise and lower your arms to show when the melody moves upward, downward, or stays the same. If you know the tune, whistle along with the music.

THEME AND VARIATIONS

In the orchestral version of "The Girl I Left Behind Me" you will hear the theme several times. It will sound different each time.

● Listen for the theme and its variations.

 "The Girl I Left Behind Me" from *Irish Suite* by Leroy Anderson

Below is the original melody. The shaded portions are sections of the melody that are changed to form the variations.

● Listen to the recording again. How did the composer vary these parts?

The Girl I Left Behind Me

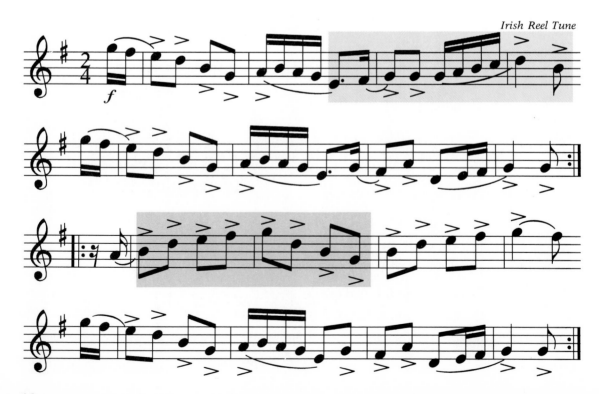

Irish Reel Tune

LEROY ANDERSON

Leroy Anderson (1908–1975) was an American composer and conductor known for his light orchestral music. His early musical training was from his mother, who was an organist. After graduating from Harvard University, Anderson became the conductor of the Harvard University Band. He later became an arranger for the Boston Pops orchestra. In 1939 he wrote his first successful composition, *Jazz Pizzicato.* He was the composer of the variations on the tune "The Girl I Left Behind Me."

WORKING TO THE TEMPO

A **sea chantey** (pronounced shan-tee) was sung by sailors to help them work together keeping the beat as they hoisted sails, pulled in or let out the anchor, or loaded heavy cargo. Chanteys were also sung for entertainment and fun in the evening.

It was very important that each work chantey be sung at the correct **tempo** or speed of the beat. One sailor, called the chantey man, knew which songs were best for each task and just how fast to sing them. Leading the singing was often the chantey man's only responsibility.

Sailors sang **short haul chanteys** while pulling ropes when only a few short pulls were needed. The chantey man sang the lines marked **call,** often making up new verses to amuse his listeners. The rest of the crew sang only the lines marked **response** as they pulled together on the strong beats.

● Listen to "Haul Away, Joe" which is a short haul chantey. Pull an imaginary rope on the strong beats of the response lines.

Haul Away, Joe

Traditional Sea Chantey
Text adapted by Robyn Lee

1. When I was just a ti - ny lad, my dear old moth - er told me,
2. So, when I kiss'd a pre - tty girl, I would have liked to tar - ry,

Way, haul a - way, we'll haul a - way, Joe,

That if I nev - er kiss'd a girl my lips would go all mold - y,
But girls don't want to kiss and run; they all would like to mar - ry.

Way, haul a - way, we'll haul a - way, Joe.

Sailors sang a **capstan chantey** while turning a large device called a capstan. It was used to raise and lower the anchor.

"Shenandoah" was sung to accompany the steady pushing movement needed to turn the capstan.

● Listen to "Shenandoah," a capstan chantey. How is its tempo different from "Haul Away, Joe"?

Shenandoah

American Sea Chantey

Solo
Oh, Shen - an - doah, I long to hear you,

Group
A - way, _____ you roll - ing riv - er.

Solo
Oh, Shen - an - doah, I long to hear you.

Group
A - way, ___ we're bound a - way, 'Cross the wide ___ Mis - sou - ri. ___

2. Oh, Shenandoah, I love your daughter.
   (Away, you rolling river.)
   Oh, Shenandoah, I love your daughter.
   (Away, I'm bound away,
   'Cross the wide Missouri.)

3. O, Shenandoah, I'm bound to leave you.
   (Away, you rolling river.)
   Oh, Shenandoah, I'll not deceive you.
   (Away, I'm bound away,
   'Cross the wide Missouri.)

14

Forecastle (pronounced foke-sull) **chanteys** were named for the part of the ship where the sailors gathered in the evenings. Sailors sang these chanteys for fun and recreation.

- Listen to this forecastle chantey dance song. How would you describe this tempo?

Going to Boston

American Sea Chantey

Ⓐ **Verse**

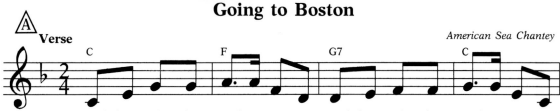

1. Good - bye girls, I'm goin' to Bos - ton, Good - bye girls, I'm goin' to Bos - ton,
2. Clear the way, you'll get run o - ver, Clear the way, you'll get run o - ver,

Good - bye girls, I'm goin' to Bos - ton, ear - ly in the morn - ing.
Clear the way, you'll get run o - ver, ear - ly in the morn - ing.

Ⓑ **Refrain**

Won't we look pret - ty in the ball-room? Won't we look pret - ty in the ball-room?

Won't we look pret - ty in the ball - room? Ear - ly in the morn - ing.

3. Saddle up, girls, and we'll go with them,
   Saddle up, girls, and we'll go with them,
   Saddle up, girls, and we'll go with them,
   Early in the morning.

ANOTHER KIND OF CHANTEY

This song is called **long-haul** or **halyard chantey.** It was sung for long jobs, such as hoisting the large sails. The chantey man sang the solos at just the right tempo, joined by the crew on the chorus part.

● Imitate a sailor hoisting a sail as you listen to "Away for Rio."

Away for Rio

American Sea Chantey

A Solo

1. Oh, the an-chor is weighed and the sails they are set,
2. We've a jol-ly good ship and a jol-ly good crew,
3. Oh, __ say, were you ev-er in Ri - o Grande?

Group

A - way _____ for Ri - o!

Solo

The gals that we're leav-ing we'll nev-er for-get,
A jol-ly good mate and a good skip-per, too,
It's there that the riv-ers run down gold-en sand,

Group

For we're bound for Ri - o Grande! _____

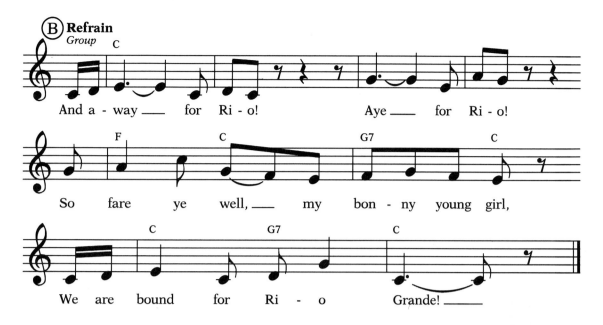

And a - way —— for Ri - o! Aye —— for Ri - o!

So fare ye well, —— my bon - ny young girl,

We are bound for Ri - o Grande! ——

C, D, and E are the first three notes in "Away for Rio."

● Find where these pitches appear in the song.

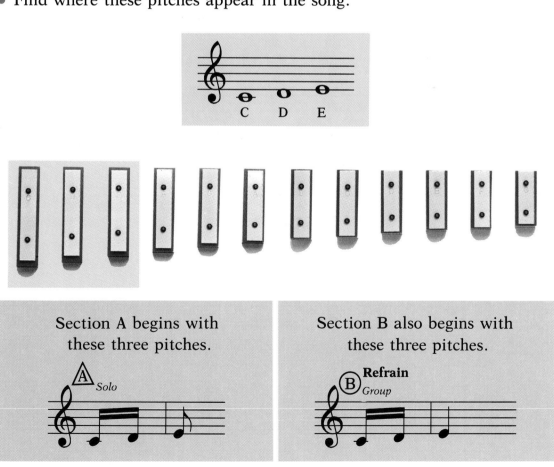

Section A begins with these three pitches.

Section B also begins with these three pitches.

● How is the A section different from the B section?

A WORKING RHYTHM

The quarter note (♩) sounds for one beat in this song. The quarter rest (𝄽) stands for one beat of silence.

- Practice these two patterns a few times. Then, do the first pattern with the verse and the second with the refrain.

Verse ‖: ♩ 𝄽 ♩ 𝄽 :‖   **Refrain** ‖: ♩ ♩ ♩ ♩ :‖

pat (wait) pat (wait)   pat clap pat clap

Erie Canal

American Work Song

1. I got a mule, her name is Sal, Fif-teen miles on the E-rie Ca-nal! _ She's a good old work-er and a good old pal, Fif-teen miles on the E-rie Ca-nal! _ We've hauled some barg-es in our day, Filled with lum-ber, coal and hay, And we know ev-ery inch of the way From Al-ba-ny _ to _ Buf-fa-lo. _____

2. Git up there, Sal, we passed that lock, Fif-teen miles on the E-rie Ca-nal! _ And _ we'll make Rome _ 'fore_ six o-'clock, Fif-teen miles on the E-rie Can-al! _ Just one more trip and back we'll go Through the rain and sleet and snow, 'Cause we know ev-ery inch of the way From Al-ba-ny _ to _ Buf-fa-lo. _____

Ⓑ **Refrain**

Low bridge, ev-'ry-bod-y down, Low bridge, 'cause we're com-ing to a town;

And you'll al-ways know your neigh-bor, You'll al-ways know your pal,

If you ev-er nav-i-gat-ed on the E-rie Ca-nal. _

The ***fermata*** (𝄐) means that the note under it is to be held longer than one beat.

- How did the *fermata* affect the way you sang "Erie Canal"?

Detail, *Junction of the Erie and Northern Canals,* J. Hill, NEW-YORK HISTORICAL SOCIETY.

The Erie Canal was opened in 1825. People and goods were moved along the canal from Albany to Buffalo. The boats were pulled by a mule which walked along the side of the canal. The mule drivers often sang to pass the long hours.

A SONG OF THE SHAKERS

The Shakers were a religious group who lived in northern New York and New England. This Shaker song praises the simple life.

Remember that either a quarter note (♩) or two eighth notes (♫) are one beat long in this song.

Simple Gifts

Shaker Song

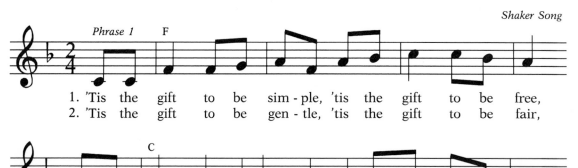

1. 'Tis the gift to be sim - ple, 'tis the gift to be free,
2. 'Tis the gift to be gen - tle, 'tis the gift to be fair,

'Tis the gift to come down where we ought to be.
'Tis the gift to wake and breathe the morn - ing air.

And when we find our - selves in the place just right,
And ev - 'ry day to walk in the path we choose,

'Twill be in the val - ley of love and de - light.
'Tis the gift that we pray we may ne'er come to lose.

Refrain

Phrase 3

F

When true sim - pli - ci - ty is gained,

To bow and to bend we shan't be a - shamed.

Phrase 4 F

To turn, turn will be our de - light,

C   F

Till by turn - ing, turn - ing we come round right.

3. 'Tis the gift to be loving, 'tis the best gift of all
   Like a quiet rain, it blesses where it falls;
   And if we have the gift, we will truly believe
   'Tis better to give than it is to receive.
   Refrain

A FAMOUS THEME AND VARIATIONS

You are a composer who is writing a new composition for an orchestra. You want to use the melody of "Simple Gifts" as your theme. The first time your plan is to use the melody in its original form. You realize that it would not be interesting to hear it four more times in exactly the same way.

● Plan four ways to vary the melody.

Aaron Copland used "Simple Gifts" as a theme for a set of variations in *Appalachian Spring*.

● See if you can tell the ways that he changed the melody as you listen to *Appalachian Spring*.

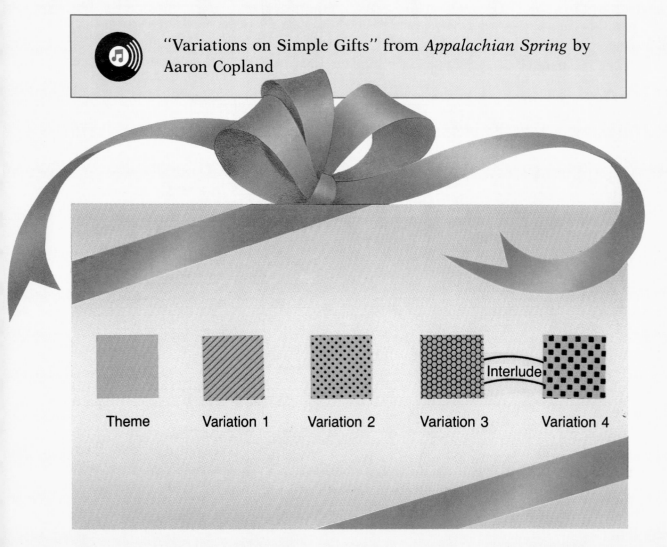

"Variations on Simple Gifts" from *Appalachian Spring* by Aaron Copland

Theme   Variation 1   Variation 2   Variation 3   Interlude   Variation 4

FOCUS ON

Aaron Copland

Aaron Copland (kō'plənd), born in Brooklyn, New York, in 1900, is one of the best known and highly respected American composers of this century. While studying piano as an eight-year-old child, he showed unusual ability by composing his first song. By the age of fifteen, he had already decided to become a composer.

In 1921, he went to France to study with the famous composition teacher Nadia Boulanger. Three years later, he returned home and continued his profession as a composer.

In his orchestral pieces, Mr. Copland used many American folk tunes so that his music could be recognized for its true American sound.

 Interview with Aaron Copland (1987)

23

AN EARLY DANCE TUNE

This song, first popular in English music halls, is often used for square dancing. Someone who seems as out of place as a marine riding a horse on board ship might be called a "horse marine."

Captain Jinks

Traditional Dance Tune

1. I'm Cap-tain Jinks of the Horse Ma-rines; I feed my horse on corn and beans, And sport young la-dies in their teens, Though a cap-tain in the Ar-my. I teach young la-dies how to dance, How to dance, how to dance, I teach young la-dies

how to dance, For I'm the pet of the Ar - my,

Refrain

I'm — Cap - tain Jinks of the Horse Ma - rines;

I feed my horse on corn and beans, And of - ten live

be - yond the means Of a Cap - tain in the Ar - my.

TAKE ANOTHER LOOK

An American Music Sampler

The American beat and the American spirit—past and present—are carried on through our music. Many of the qualities that are part of our national character have been present from the beginning of our country. These qualities show clearly in our songs.

Our good humor was evident from the beginning, when a song that was composed to make fun of us became one of our all-time favorites. (Sing "Yankee Doodle.")

The imagination of our sailors is shown in songs that were made up to make the difficult work of sailing the great clipper ships easier. (Sing "Haul Away, Joe," "Shenandoah," "Going to Boston," and "Away for Rio.")

The honest hard-working spirit that built America was expressed in the songs of the early settlers again and again. (Sing "Simple Gifts.")

Most of all, the love we have for our country shows in our music. Through it the American beat, the American spirit, has gone on—and always will. (Sing "This Land Is Your Land.")

JUST CHECKING

1. Which note is on the strong beat in each measure?

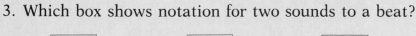

2. Which box shows notation for one sound to a beat?

   a. [♩]   b. [𝄽]   c. [♫]

3. Which box shows notation for two sounds to a beat?

   a. [♩]   b. [𝄽]   c. [♫]

4. Which box shows notation for no sounds to a beat?

   a. [♩]   b. [𝄽]   c. [♫]

5. Which set of letters shows the form of a song that has two different sections?
   a. AA   b. AB

6. Which set of letters shows the form of a song that has two sections that are the same?
   a. AA   b. AB

UNIT 2 SINGING AMERICA AT WORK AND PLAY

In nineteenth century America, music was such an important part of life that there was a song for almost every occasion.

"American Songs
for Work
and Play"

SONGS FOR WORK AND PLAY

Nothing did more to help the expansion of our country than the newly developed train system. The "Iron Horse," as the locomotive engine was called, was a symbol of great power.

The sound of the engine, the bell, and the whistle inspired many songs, poems, pictures, and stories. "The Wabash Cannonball" is thought to be such a song.

- Listen to "The Wabash Cannonball." Clap on the first and third beats as you sing the verses. Clap only on the strong (first) beat during each refrain.

American Express Train, print by Currier and Ives

The Wabash Cannonball

Music by William Kindt
Words adapted by M.S.

1. From the waves of the At-lan-tic to the wild Pa-ci-fic shore,
Refrain Now—— lis-ten to her rum-ble, now — lis-ten to her roar,

From the coast of Cal-i-for-nia to snow-bound La-bra-dor,
As she ech-oes down the val-ley and flies a-long the shore.

There's a train of fan-cy lay-out that's well known to us all,
Now — hear the en-gine whis-tle, It's a might-y lone-some call.

It's the ho-bo's home when he wants to roam—It's the Wa-bash Can-non-ball.
As we ride the bars and the emp-ty cars——on the Wa-bash Can-non-ball.

2. There's lots of places, partner, that you can go to see.
   St. Paul and Kansas City, Des Moines and Kankakee,
   From the lakes of Minnehaha where the laughing waters fall,
   You reach them by no other than the Wabash Cannonball.

3. For years I've ridden on this line across the countryside.
   I've always been well treated, tho' I took the hobo's ride.
   And when my days are over, and the curtains 'round me fall,
   Please ship me off to Heaven on the Wabash Cannonball.

Diminuendo (də-min-yə-wen'dō) means "getting gradually softer." It means the same as **decrescendo** (dā-krə-shen'dō).

● Listen to the "Wabash Cannonball" again for the recorded *diminuendo* in the instrumental ending. What is the effect that it creates?

In the early days of our country, street musicians often sang for people passing by. They accompanied themselves on instruments such as the banjo. "Banjo Sam" is one of the songs they sang.

- Find these three pitches in the verse of this song.

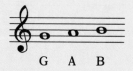

G A B

- Are there any other pitches in the verse?

Banjo Sam

North Carolina Folk Song

2. As I was goin' through the field,
   A black snake bit me on the heel.
   I grabbed a stick and done my best,
   And ran my head in a hornet's nest.
   Refrain

3. As I was goin' down the road,
   I met a terrapin and a toad.
   The terrapin, he began to sing,
   The toad, he cut the pigeon-wing.
   Refrain

TONAL CENTER

Many times music seems to center around a pitch. The pitch acts as if it were a magnet. It is often the last note in a song. The melody tends to return to home base or a resting place. This is the **tonal center.**

Billy, Billy

Texas Folk Song

1. Here's the way we Bil - ly, Bil - ly, Bil - ly, Bil - ly, Bil - ly, Bil - ly,
2. Step __ back, __ Sal - ly! ___ Step __ back, __ Sal - ly! ___

Here's the way we Bil - ly, Bil - ly, all night long.
Step ___ back, ___ Sal - ly, ___ all night long!

3. Struttin' down the alley! Struttin' down the alley!
   Struttin' down the alley, all night long!

4. Here comes another one, just like the other one.
   Here comes another one, all night long!

• Find the pitch that is the tonal center of "Billy, Billy."

- Find this pitch in the song below.
- Is it the tonal center?

F

Rolling Power by Charles Sheeler

Jubilee

Kentucky Singing Game

1. All out on the old rail-road, All out on the sea;
All out on the old rail-road As far as I could see.

Refrain
Swing and turn, Ju - bi - lee, Live and learn, Ju - bi - lee.

2. Hardest work I ever done:
Working on the farm.
Easiest work I ever done
Was swing my true love's arm.
Refrain

3. If I had no horse at all
I'd be found a-crawlin'
Up and down this rocky road
Lookin' for my darlin'.
Refrain

4. All I want's a big fat horse
Corn to feed it on,
Pretty little girl to stay at home
And feed it when I'm gone.
Refrain

These are the pitches high
C and high D.

- Play this harmony part on high C and high D for the verse of "Jubilee."

C   D   C   D   D   C
Ju - bi - lee!   Ju - bi - lee!

You can play the same pattern using these
pitches C and D. They are one **octave**
(eight steps) below high C
and high D.

- Play this harmony part on C and D for the verse of "Jubilee."

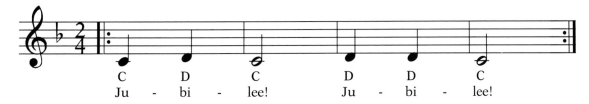

C   D   C   D   D   C
Ju - bi - lee!   Ju - bi - lee!

WORK SONGS OF THE RAILROAD

New Americans from Ireland and China did much of the work in building the railroads across the United States. Building the railroad was difficult and dangerous. Supplies were scarce. Life in the wilderness was hard. It took great courage to do this job.

The following song was written by two Irish-Americans. They later performed it on the stage. It tells about some of the hardships these railroad builders faced.

Drill, Ye Tarriers

Words and music by
Thomas Casey and Charles Connolly

1. Oh, ev-'ry morn-in' at sev-en o' clock, There's a hun-dred tar-ri-ers a-work-in' at the rock And the boss comes a-long and he says, "Keep still! And come down heav-y on the cast iron drill," and

2. Now, our new fore-man was Jer-ry Mc-Cann, You can bet that he was sure a blame mean man, Last week a pre-ma-ture blast went off, And a mile in the air went big Jim Goff, and

3. Now, next time pay-day come a-round, Jim Goff a dol-lar short was found, When asked what for, came this re-ply, "You were docked for the time you were up in the sky!" So

Refrain

Drill, ye tar-ri-ers, drill. Drill, ye tar-ri-ers, drill. Oh, it's work all day for sug-ar in your tay, Down be-hind the rail-way, Oh, drill, ye tar-ri-ers, drill!

- Read this poem with expression. Use vocal tone color to show the drama and excitement of a speeding steam engine.

A Modern Dragon

A train is a dragon that roars through the dark.
He wriggles his tail as he sends up a spark.
He pierces the night with his one yellow eye,
And all the earth trembles as he rushes by.

—*Rowena Bastin Bennett*

The "Pacific 231" was a type of American locomotive used all over the world. It had six wheels on each side; two wheels together, then three large wheels, then one single wheel.

Pacific 231 was composed by Arthur Honegger. In this symphonic work, he used the instruments of the orchestra to re-create the sounds of these huge, spectacular engines.

Arthur Honegger (hän'i-gər) was born in France in 1892. As a young boy, he spent hours watching boats and trains at the harbor. The locomotive was the inspiration for his piece *Pacific 231*. He attended the Paris Conservatory and studied under many famous musicians. Honneger's works include operas, chamber music, and orchestral, vocal, and choral music.

● Look at and listen to each of these themes.

Theme 1

Theme 2

Theme 3

Theme 4

Pacific 231 by Arthur Honegger

EXPRESS YOURSELF!

Make up your own train music with a group from your class. First, think about the sounds that trains or people building railroads make. Re-create these sounds with instruments or objects, such as a wastepaper basket, found in the classroom.

Decide on what kind of effect you and your group want to create. Try to use a *crescendo* or a *diminuendo*. **Crescendo** (krə-shen'dō) means getting gradually louder.

Write down your music to share with others. Use quarter notes (♩), and eighth notes (♪ or ♫), and any other symbols that will make it easier to read and remember. Practice your composition and perform it for the rest of the class.

The completion of the transcontinental railroad in 1869 ended an important era of American history. The wilderness, including the vast untouched buffalo country, would soon be gone.

Buffalo and Elk on the Upper Missouri by Karl Bodmer

Detail *Buffalo and Elk on the Upper Missouri*, Karl Bodmer.

Buffalo Dusk

The buffaloes are gone.
And those who saw the buffaloes are gone.
Those who saw the buffaloes by thousands and
    how they pawed the prairie sod into dust
    with their hoofs, their great heads down
    pawing on in a great pageant of dusk,
Those who saw the buffaloes are gone.
And the buffaloes are gone.

                 —*Carl Sandburg*

● Use a variety of tone colors to read this poem.

GHOSTLY RHYTHM PATTERNS

- What pitch is the home base or tonal center in this song?

The Ghost of John

Words and music by Martha Grubb

Have you seen the ghost of John?

Long white bones with the skin all gone, ____

Oo, oo ____

Would-n't it be chil-ly with no skin on!

- Find the *crescendo* (◁) and *diminuendo* (▷) signs in "The Ghost of John." How do these signs affect the way you sing this song?

These rhythms contain **whole notes** (o), **half notes** (♩),
quarter notes (♩), and eighth notes (♫).

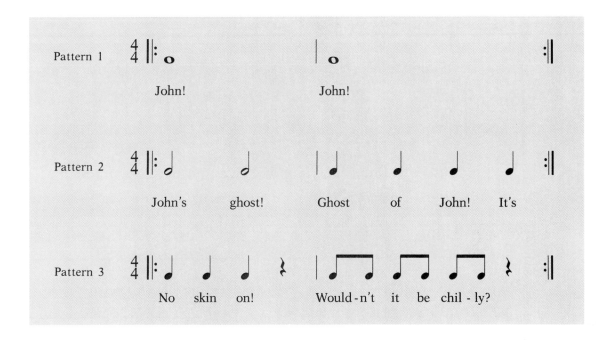

- In these examples, how long does a whole note sound?
  How long does a half note sound? Which note sounds for a
  longer time?
- Practice saying and clapping the rhythms above separately.
  Choose a different instrument to play each pattern.
  Combine the patterns. Play them over and over, adding one
  pattern at a time.

The music to *Danse Macabre* was written to suggest a story.

Danse Macabre by Camille Saint-Saëns

● Listen to *Danse Macabre*. As you listen, follow the picture
trail around the edges of these two pages. Decide what you
think the story might be. The pictures go with the music.

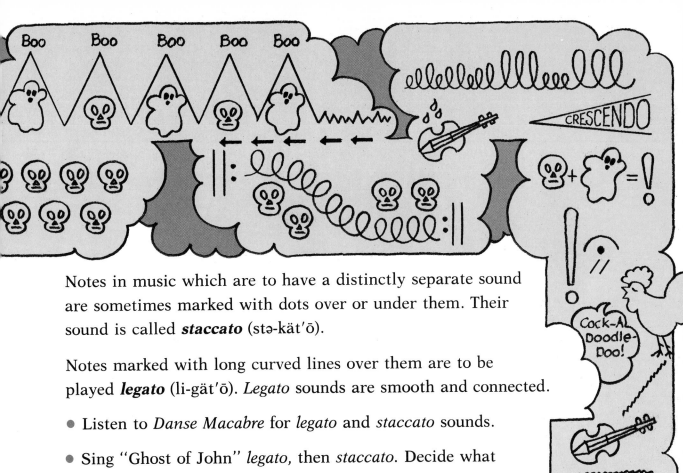

Notes in music which are to have a distinctly separate sound are sometimes marked with dots over or under them. Their sound is called **staccato** (stə-kät′ō).

Notes marked with long curved lines over them are to be played **legato** (li-gät′ō). *Legato* sounds are smooth and connected.

- Listen to *Danse Macabre* for *legato* and *staccato* sounds.

- Sing "Ghost of John" *legato*, then *staccato*. Decide what effect is created each time.

CAMILLE .. SAINT-SAËNS

Camille Saint-Saëns (kä-mē-yə saN-säNs) was born in Paris on October 9, 1835. He began his musical career as a composer and concert pianist when he was just a child. For many years he played the organ at the famous Madeleine Church in Paris. By the time he was 22, he was a famous composer. *Danse Macabre* is one of his most popular pieces.

45

SINGING WITH EXPRESSION

● Look and listen for the tonal center in this song.

The Boogie Woogie Ghost

Words and music by Nadine M. Peglar

1. There was a ghost on Hal-low-een, He real-ly made the ghost-ie scene,
2. He'd go out spook-ing late at night, And giv-ing ev-ery-one a fright,

He was the Boo-gie-Woo-gie Ghost, He was the ghost-ie with the most,
He knew some wit-ches, two or three, And they would all go on a spree,

And when the kid-dies came a-round, He'd give out with a ghost-ly sound,
And when the morn-ing came a-round, He'd give one last mys-te-rious sound,

He'd go, ___ "Boo - oo - oo - oo - ooo."
He'd go, ___ "Boo - oo - oo - oo - ooo."

46

Though he real-ly was-n't ver-y spook-y, ___ Kids all thought that he was rath-er

cool.   E - ven though he was   a lit - tle kook - y, ___

He was just   a spe - cial _   ghoul.   When you're out   on Hal - low-een

And he ap-pears up - on the scene, Don't give   a scream and run   a-way,

Just ask him if he'll stay and play. You'll like   the Boo - gie-Woo - gie Ghost,

He'll be the one you dig   the most, You'll love his Boo - oo - oo-oo - GOO.

TAKE ANOTHER LOOK

Singing America at Work and Play

Americans love music. They enjoy it whether they are at their jobs, at home, or away, no matter what the occasion.

Whether you're a train worker or a passenger, a song like "The Wabash Cannonball" is fun to sing. (Sing "The Wabash Cannonball.")

Everyone loves to hear and sing songs of street musicians, and "Banjo Sam" is no exception. (Sing "Banjo Sam.")

People of all ages can have fun dancing and singing with songs like "Billy, Billy" and "Jubilee." (Sing "Billy, Billy" and "Jubilee.")

Even getting a little scared can be fun with the right song to sing. (Sing "The Ghost of John.")

JUST CHECKING

1. Which note is a whole note?

   a. 𝅗𝅥   b. 𝅝

2. Which note is a half note?

   a. 𝅗𝅥   b. 𝅝

3. Which note represents the longer sound?

   a. 𝅗𝅥   b. 𝅝

4. Which word means to get gradually softer?
   a. minor   b. tempo
   c. *crescendo*   d. *diminuendo*

5. What is the tonal center in the song "The Boogie Woogie Ghost" on page 46?

6. What is the tonal center in the song "The Wabash Cannonball" on page 31?

7. What is the musical symbol for *diminuendo?*
   a. ⟨   b. ⟩

8. In this example, how long does a half note sound?

9. In this example, how long does a whole note sound?

UNIT 3

THE AMERICAN BEAT MOVES WEST!

In the mid-1800s, Americans moved west in large numbers. Their rhythmic music was like the pioneer people themselves—strongly accented, energetic, restless, down-to-earth, and full of life!

● Listen to this country fiddle music, which was very popular.

 "Cindy," American Folk Tune

MOVING IN TEMPO

- Listen to "Cindy." Move to the beat as you listen. Decide if the speed of the beat in this version is faster or slower than the way the fiddler played it.

Cindy

Appalachian Folk Song

1. I wish I was an ap-ple a-hang-ing on a tree,
and ev-'ry time my Cin-dy passed she'd take a bite of me!

Refrain

Get a-long home, Cin-dy Cin-dy, get a-long home Cin-dy Cin-dy,
get a-long home, Cin-dy Cin-dy, I'll mar-ry you — some-day.

2. She told me that she loved me,
   She called me sugar plum,
   She threw her arms around me
   And I thought my time had come.

3. I wish I had a needle
   As fine as I could sew,
   I'd sew that gal to my coattail,
   And down the road I'd go.

52

Music should be performed at the tempo the composer intended. Composers indicate the tempo by using special Italian words at the beginning of their music. These words are understood all over the world.

Here are three common terms for tempo with their English meanings.

allegro—fast
presto—very fast
lento–slow

- If you had composed the fiddle version of "Cindy," which Italian tempo marking would you have put on the music? Which would you have used for the song, "Cindy"?

- Listen to another version of "Cindy" played by an orchestra. Identify the tempos you hear, using the terms *allegro*, *presto*, and *lento*.

 "Cindy" from *Kentucky Mountain Portraits* by Lyndol Mitchell

Taking care of motherless calves, called dogies (pronounced doh-geez) was an important part of the cowhands' job. The cowhands often sang quietly to the dogies to help calm them.

● What musical tempo term would best fit this song?

Git Along, Little Dogies

American Cowboy Song

Ⓐ **Phrase 1**

p   C   F   G7   C

1. As   I   was a - walk - ing   one   morn - ing   for   pleas - ure,
2. Now   ear - ly   in   spring - time   we   round up   the   do - gies,
3. It's   whoop - ing and yell - ing   and   driv - ing   the   do - gies,

                    F   G7   C

I   spied   a   cow - punch - er   a - rid - ing   a - long;
We   mark   them and   brand them   and   bob   off   their tails;
Oh,   how   I   wish   you ___   would   go   right   a - long;

C   F   G7   C

His   hat   was thrown back and   his   spurs were   a - jing - lin',
We   drive   up   our   hors - es   and   load   the chuck wag - on,
It's whoop - ing and punch - ing, git   on,   lit - tle   do - gies,

                    F   G7   C

And   as   he   ap - proached he   was   sing - ing   this   song.
Then   throw ___   the   do - gies   out   on - to   the   trail.
You   know   that Wy - o - ming   will   be   your   new   home.

B **Refrain**

B♭   C   F

Whoop - ee ti - yi - yo, git a - long, lit - tle do - gies.

B♭   C   F   C

It's your mis - for - tune and none of my own;

C   F   G7   C

Whoop - ee ti - yi - yo, git al - long, lit - tle do - gies,

C   F   G7   C

You know that Wy - o - ming will be your new home.

LISTENING FOR LOUD AND SOFT

- Listen and move to this song in a way that will show that you hear the phrase that has a different melody. Is this phrase as loud as the other phrases?
- Sing this song with energy, but be careful not to sing too loudly.

Cumberland Mountain Bear Chase

Presto

American Folk Song

Refrain

f A - way, a - way, we're bound for the moun - tain,

bound for the moun - tain, bound for the moun - tain!

O - ver the hill, the fields and the foun - tain,

a - way, to the chase, a - way, a - way.

Verse

1. Now we're set just right for the race, the
2. Rov - er, Rov - er, see him,____ see him,
3. Lis-ten to the hound dog's heav - y____ bay,____
4. All night long till break of____ dawn,____

old hound dogs are read - y for the chase,
Rov - er, Rov - er, catch __ him, __ catch him,
Sound - ing high____ o - ver the way,
Mer - ri - ly the chase __ goes __ on,

O - ver the moun - tain, the fields and the foun - tain, a -

way to the chase a - - way, a - way.

- Find the dynamic markings, *f* and *p*, in this song.

f is an abbreviation for **forte** (loud).
p is an abbreviation for **piano** (soft).

- Listen to music that has sudden changes in dynamics.

"Bear Dance" by Béla Bartók

You have already used the terms *piano* (soft) and *forte* (loud) in "Cumberland Mountain Bear Chase."

> The term for very soft is **pianissimo.**
> Its abbreviation is ***pp***
>
> The term for very loud is **fortissimo.**
> Its abbreviation is ***ff***

● Listen again to Bartók's "Bear Dance." Decide what the order of the dynamic markings might be.

The Pioneer's Home on the Western Frontier, print by Currier and Ives

● Sing this song. Follow the tempo markings.

Great Grand-dad

American Folk Song

1. Great Grand - dad, when the land was young, _____
2. Twenty - one chil - dren _____ came to bless The
3. Great Grand - dad was a bus - y man, _____

Barred the door with a wag - on tongue,
old man's home in the wil - der - ness.
Cooked his grub in a fry - ing pan,

For the times was rough and the red - skins mocked,
They _____ slept on the floor with the dogs and cats,
He _____ picked his teeth with his hunt - ing knife,

And he said his prayers with his shot - gun cocked.
And they hunt-ed in the woods in their coon - skin caps.
And he wore the same suit _____ all his life.

MOVE TO THE STRONG BEAT

This painting shows the trust necessary between a cowhand and his horse. The horse and rider worked together to round up cattle.

The Cow Puncher
by Frederick Remington

Try to imagine the feelings of the cowhand who must say
good-bye to his horse in this song.

● How can these feelings be shown in the tempo?

Good-Bye, Old Paint

American Folk Song

Refrain *mp* F ... C7 ... F

Good - bye, Old Paint, I'm a - leav - in' Chey - enne,

F ... C7 ... F

Good - bye, Old Paint, I'm a - leav - in' Chey - enne.

Verse F ... C7 ... F

1. I'm a - leav - in' Chey - enne, I'm off for Mon - tan', ___
2. Old ___ Paint's a good po-ny, He pac - es when he can, ___

F ... C7 ... F

Good - bye, Old Paint, I'm a - leav - in' Chey - enne.
Good morning, young lady, My ___ hors - es won't stand.

Many American Indian games require coordination and precise rhythm.

- Play the Paiute stick game. Do this pattern as you sing.

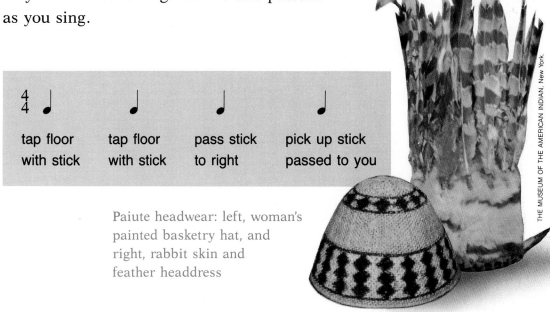

| tap floor with stick | tap floor with stick | pass stick to right | pick up stick passed to you |

Paiute headwear: left, woman's painted basketry hat, and right, rabbit skin and feather headdress

THE MUSEUM OF THE AMERICAN INDIAN, New York.

Paiute Stick Game Song

Paiute Indian Song

Ha ni no —— wi ya ha ni no wi ya

ha ni no —— wi ya ha ni no

wi ya ha ni no —— wi ya ha ni no

wi ya ha ni no —— wi ya ha ni no

Paiute Stick Game

NATIVE AMERICAN ARTS

Navajo sand paintings are created with colored sand. The designs are usually very detailed and are often completed in one day. The Navajo people have kept their traditions and legends alive through the sand paintings.

These are examples of Navajo sand paintings used in a ceremony for healing the sick. The medicine man made the sand paintings before the ceremony began, using different symbols depending on the patient's illness. The sand paintings were thought to attract the spirits necessary to cure the patient.

"Loneliness Song" is believed to have been first sung in 1864 by an unknown Navajo woman. It shows the Navajo's search for beauty in all aspects of life.

● What dynamic level would be appropriate for this song?

Loneliness Song

Navajo Indian Song

Allegro

As ____ I walk, as ____ I walk,
She ____ na' sha, she ____ na' sha,

As ____ I walk, O may my path be beau-ti - ful for me.
She ____ na' sha, B' keh, huh zho-la he-yah heyn' neh' yuh.

Or I'm a-lone in my lone - li - ness. ____
Ah' ah' luh, ah' ah' luh koh' nuh sha. ____

65

THE BEAT IN $\frac{4}{4}$ METER

Meter in music refers to how beats are grouped.

Music in $\frac{4}{4}$ meter has this combination of strong and weak beats.

      strong - weak - medium strong - weak

• Show the beats in $\frac{4}{4}$ by using this pattern.

      pat - clap - snap - clap

Remember to clap very lightly so that these are the softest sounds.

Come, Ye Thankful People, Come

Music by Sir George Job Elvey
Words by Henry Alford

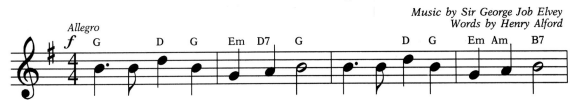

1. Come, ye thank-ful peo-ple, come, Raise the song of har-vest home:
2. All the world is God's own field, Fruit un-to his praise to yield;

All is safe-ly gath-ered in Ere the win-ter storms be-gin;
Wheat and tares to-geth-er sown, Un-to joy or sor-row grown;

God, our Mak-er, doth pro-vide For our wants to be sup-plied;
First the blade, and then the ear, Then the full corn shall ap-pear;

Come to God's own tem-ple, come, Raise the song of har-vest home.
Lord of har-vest, grant that we Whole-some grain and pure may be.

• Sing the louder parts of this song with more energy.

Summer by Abel Grimmer

A THANKSGIVING ROUND

- Identify the meter of this song.
- Sing "For Thy Gracious Blessings." Watch for and use tempo and dynamic markings that are given.

For Thy Gracious Blessings

Traditional Melody
Arranged by M.C.D.
Words by Lester S. Bucher

For Thy gra-cious bless-ings, For Thy won-drous Word.

For Thy lov-ing kind-ness We give thanks, Oh Lord.

- Sing "For Thy Gracious Blessings" as a two-part round.
  One group begins when the other gets to the 2.

A **descant** is a different melody, often higher, sung with a song.

- Sing or play this descant with "For Thy Gracious Blessings."

For Thy gra-cious bless-ings, For Thy won-drous word,

For Thy lov-ing kind-ness, We give thanks, Oh Lord.

68

Home to Thanksgiving, print by Currier and Ives

This picture by Currier and Ives expresses the dream of going home for the holidays.

- Do you think many of the pioneers dreamt this dream at holiday time?

TAKE ANOTHER LOOK

The American Beat Moves West!

The "Frontier Days" in American history extended over a long period of time. The frontiers were constantly changing as people moved deeper and deeper into the wilderness.

In 1769, Daniel Boone took his first group of settlers through the Cumberland Gap in the Appalachian Mountains. They made their way through this pass, braving all sorts of dangers and, of course, bragging about it in song. (Sing "Great Grand-dad" and "Cumberland Mountain Bear Chase.")

The early settlers worked very hard, but no people loved to have a good time any more than they did. One song that was popular at their parties was "Cindy." (Sing "Cindy.")

As the frontier was pushed west, another hero appeared—the cowboy. The cowboy hero of legends is gone. However, he still lives on in the songs that were written by him and about him. (Sing "Git Along, Little Dogies.")

Thanksgiving did not officially become a national holiday until 1863, but an autumn harvest celebration has always been an American tradition. Whatever our own traditions might be, we can all share with each other a feeling of gratitude for the good things in our lives. (Sing "Come, Ye Thankful People, Come.")

JUST CHECKING

1. Which term means very loud?

   a. *fortissimo*　　　　b. *pianissimo*

2. Which term means soft?

   a. *forte*　　　　b. *piano*

3. Match each tempo term with its definition.

Tempo Terms	Definitions
1. *allegro*	a. slow
2. *lento*	b. very fast
3. *presto*	c. fast

4. Which pattern below is an example of the beat pattern in $\frac{4}{4}$ meter?

   a. strong—weak—weak—weak

   b. strong—weak—strong—weak

   c. strong—weak—medium strong—weak

5. Which term means very soft?

   a. *fortissimo*　　　　b. *pianissimo*

6. Which term means loud?

   a. *forte*　　　　b. *piano*

7. Match each term with its abbreviation.

1. *forte*	a. *pp*
2. *pianissimo*	b. *f*
3. *piano*	c. *ff*
4. *fortissimo*	d. *p*

UNIT 4 THE WINTER HOLIDAY BEAT

The people who came to live
in America brought their own holiday
music from their homelands. Their
different customs are reflected in
their music. All the songs have one
thing in common—the happy sound
of the holidays!

"Holiday Music
Montage"

SYNCOPATION:
AN EXCITING RHYTHM!

Syncopation (sing-kə-pā′shən) is a name for rhythm that has sounds or silences where you do not normally expect them.

Here is one kind of a syncopated rhythm pattern.

- Clap each rhythm pattern. A **tie** (‿) means to hold the sound for the length of both notes.

The syncopated rhythm pattern sounds the same as the tied rhythm pattern.

- Look for the syncopated pattern in "Winter Fantasy."

Print by Currier and Ives

Winter Fantasy

Words and music by Jill Gallina

- Find the syncopated rhythm in this pattern.

- Clap or play this pattern as an **ostinato** (äs-tə-nät′ō), or repeated pattern, with "O Hanukah."

O Hanukah

Jewish Folk Song

O Ha-nu-kah, O Ha-nu-kah, come light the me-no-rah!

Let's have a par-ty, we'll all dance the ho-ra.

Gath-er round the ta-ble, we'll give you a treat,

Spin-ning tops to play with, and good things to eat.

And while we are play-ing, the can-dles are burn-ing _ low

One for each night, they __ shed a sweet light

76

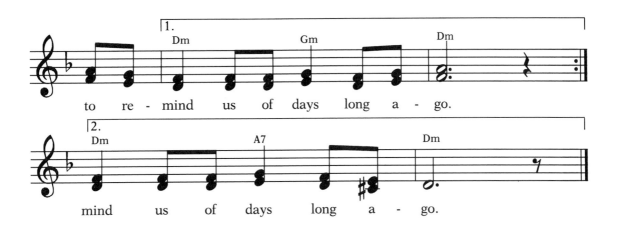

to re - mind us of days long a - go.

mind us of days long a - go.

This menorah (mə-nôr′ə), which holds candles, is one of the symbols of the celebration of Hanukah (hän′ə-kə). This holiday is sometimes called the Festival of Lights. Over 2,000 years ago, the Jewish people of Jerusalem saved their temple from their enemies. There was only a small amount of sacred oil to burn in the temple's lamps.

Amazingly this oil lasted eight days, until more oil could be prepared. Today Jewish people light candles to honor this event. The holiday lasts eight days. One candle is lit on the first night, two on the second night, and so on, until on the eighth night all eight candles are lit. The ninth candle in the center of the menorah is used to light the other candles.

MAJOR AND MINOR

For every major scale there is a related minor scale. Both scales use the same pitches, but each begins and ends on a different pitch.

- Play the bells from F to high F.
  This is the sound of a **major scale.**

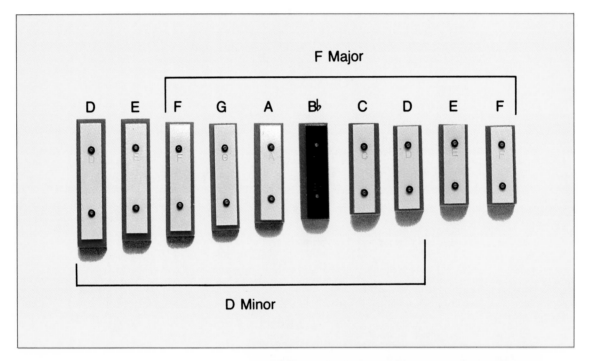

- Now play the bells from D to high D. This is the sound of **a minor scale.**

- Play both scales. Listen for the difference in the sound.

● Listen to this song and decide if it is in major or minor.

Carol from an Irish Cabin

Music by Dale Wood
Words Anonymous

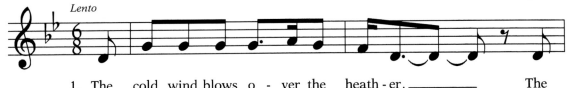

Lento

1. The cold wind blows o - ver the heath - er, _____ The
2. The clean snow falls soft - ly, falls soft - ly, _____ The
3. So let there be no fear of dark - ness, _____ And

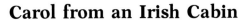

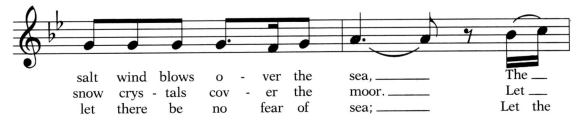

salt wind blows o - ver the sea, _____ The __
snow crys - tals cov - er the moor. _____ Let __
let there be no fear of sea; _____ Let the

harsh wind blows down from the moun - tains, ____ And
wan - der - ers lost and grown wea - ry, _____ Find
star guide the lost and for - sak - en, _____ Safe

blows a white Christ - mas to me.
wel - come at my cab - in door.
o - ver the moor - lands to me.

● Listen and decide if "Feliz Navidad" (fā-lēs' nä-vē-däd') is
in major or minor.

Feliz Navidad

Words and music by José Feliciano

80

I want to wish you a Mer-ry Christ-mas with lots of pres-ents to make you hap-py.

I want to wish you a Mer-ry Christ-mas from the bot-tom of my heart. _____

_____ I want to wish you a Mer-ry Christ-mas with mis-tle-toe and _ lots of cheer. _

D. C. al fine

With lots of laugh-ter through-out the years from the bot-tom of my heart. _____

You can clap a syncopated rhythm pattern with "Feliz Navidad."

● Find the three-note syncopated pattern in this rhythm.

● Clap this rhythm wherever it appears in this song.

Singer, songwriter, and guitarist José Feliciano

SYNCOPATED PATTERNS

● Find the clapped syncopated pattern in this song.

Mama, Bake the Johnny Cake,

Christmas Comin'

Words and music by
Blake Alphonso Higgs

- What sections do you see in this song?
- What is the form of this song, AB or ABA?

The three rhythms on this page are patterns you have been
singing, clapping, and playing.

- Find the three-note syncopated combination (♪♩ ♪) in
  each.

All o - ver town.

Wish you a good Christ - mas!

Light a light to - night!

- Write each pattern on a separate sheet of paper.
- As you listen to "Jamaican Rumba," hold up the pattern
  that you hear many times in this music.

 "Jamaican Rumba" by Arthur Benjamin

SONGS IN MAJOR AND MINOR

This carol originated in a part of France called Provence (prô-väNs'). Each year in Provence, three youths are chosen to play the kings in a procession. It is a great honor to be chosen.

● Listen for the melody in "March of the Kings." Decide if it is major or minor.

March of the Kings

French Carol

Three great kings I met at ear-ly morn,
Ce ma - tin, J'ai ren - con - tré le train

With all their ret-in-ue were slow-ly march-ing;
De trois grands Rois qui al - laient en voy - a - ge,

Three great kings I met at ear-ly morn,
Ce ma - tin, J'ai ren - con - tré le train

were on their way to meet the new-ly born.
De trois grands Rois de's - sus le grand che - min.

With gifts of gold brought from far a - way,
Tout char - gés d'or les sui - vaient d'a - bord

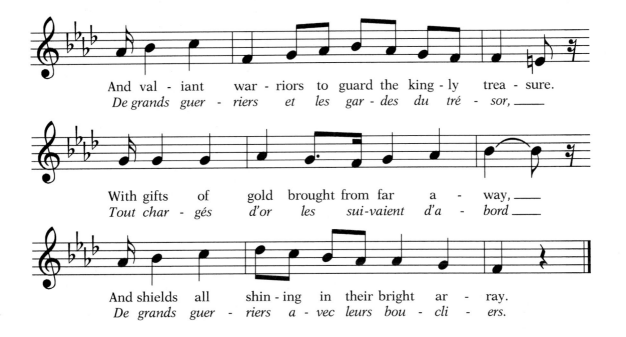

And val - iant war - riors to guard the king - ly trea - sure.
De grands guer - riers et les gar - des du tré - sor, ____

With gifts of gold brought from far a - way, ____
Tout char - gés d'or les sui - vaient d'a - bord ____

And shields all shin - ing in their bright ar - ray.
De grands guer - riers a - vec leurs bou - cli - ers.

- Play the white keys from A to A. Play the white keys from C to C.
- Which is a major sound? Which is a minor sound?

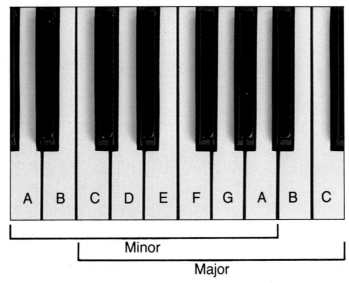

- Listen as others play. Indicate when you hear major or minor.
- Listen for major and minor in an orchestral composition that uses a melody you know.

 "Farandole," from *L'Arlésienne* by Georges Bizet

87

DYNAMIC MARKINGS

You have learned that *piano* means "soft" and *forte* means "loud." The Italian word for "medium" is **mezzo** (met′sō). Add *mezzo* to *piano* and *forte* to describe two different dynamic levels.

The term **mezzo forte (*mf*)** means "medium loud," and **mezzo piano (*mp*)** means "medium soft."

- Read this poem using a different dynamic level for each line. Decide on a plan you like. Read the poem following your plan.

Old Christmastide

Heap on more wood! —the wind is chill;
But let it whistle as it will
We'll keep our Christmas merry still.

—*Walter Scott*

Norman Rockwell illustration, from the cover of *The Saturday Evening Post*, 1928

American settlers hoped to find peace and freedom. The hope of all people for peace is expressed in "Let There Be Peace on Earth."

● Find the dynamic markings in this song. Then sing the song with expression.

Let There Be Peace on Earth

Words and music by Sy Miller and Jill Jackson

p
C   Am   F   G7   C   F   C   F   G7
Let there be peace on earth, and let it be-gin with me, ____

mp
C   Am   B7   Em   B7   G   G7
Let there be peace on earth, The peace that was meant to be. ____

mf
Am   Em   F   G7   C
With God as our Fa - ther, ____ Broth-ers all are we. ____

C   D7   G   Am   D7   G   G7
Let me walk with my broth-er ____ In per-fect har-mo-ny. ____

p *A little faster*
C   Am   F   G7   C   F   C   F   G7
Let peace be-gin with me, Let this be the mo-ment now: ____

mp   *a little slower*
C   Am   B7   Em   B7   G   G7
With ev-'ry step I take, Let this be my sol-emn vow: ____

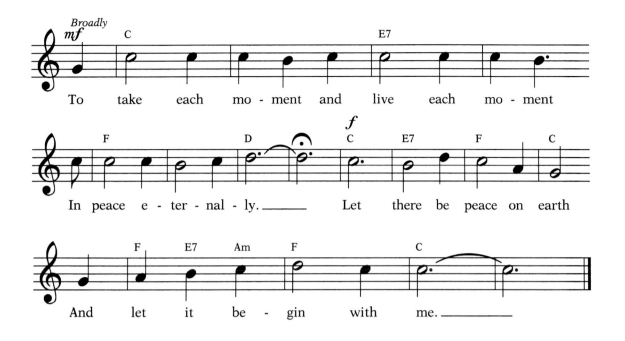

To take each mo - ment and live each mo - ment

In peace e - ter - nal - ly._____ Let there be peace on earth

And let it be - gin with me._____

HOLIDAY PARTNERS

This song has two melody parts. They are "partners" in making harmony.

● Sing this song in two groups to create harmony.

Winter Fantasy

Words and music by Jill Gallina

Part I* A mf

Snow - flakes fall - ing all o - ver town,

Part II* mf

Dash - ing through the snow in a one-horse o - pen sleigh.

slip - ping, slid - ing, ev - 'ry - bod - y rush - in' 'round.

O'er the fields we go, laugh - ing all the way.

There's an i - cy chill in the air,

Bells on bob - tails ring. mak - ing spir - its bright. What

tell - ing us that win - ter's real - ly here. Oh!

fun it is to laugh and sing a sleigh - ing song to - night. Oh!

First time: Part I only; Second time: Part II only; Third time: Parts I and II

TAKE ANOTHER LOOK

The Winter Holiday Beat

Holiday songs are fun to sing because they are happy reminders of celebrations. There is music for singing, listening, dancing, or playing games. Some holiday songs are like greeting cards. (Sing "Feliz Navidad.")

Some holiday songs help people share their heritage and culture. (Sing "O Hanukah.")

Many of our songs reflect the influence of the country from which the music originally came. (Sing "Carol from an Irish Cabin.")

Singing songs about winter holidays helps us think about this season and all the activities that are so much fun to share with our friends. (Sing "Winter Fantasy.")

No song could be more fitting at holiday time than one which expresses the hope of people everywhere for peace. (Sing "Let There Be Peace on Earth.")

JUST CHECKING

1. Which dynamic marking means medium soft?

   mf   *mp*   *p*   *ff*   *pp*

2. Which dynamic marking means medium loud?

   mf   *mp*   *p*   *ff*   *pp*

3. What is the tonal center of the song "Let There Be Peace on Earth" on page 90?

4. What is the tonal center of the song "O Hanukah" on page 76?

5. Which pattern shows syncopation?

   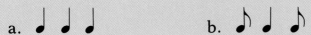

6. Which term means medium loud?

   a. *mezzo forte*   b. *mezzo piano*

7. Which term means medium soft?

   a. *mezzo forte*   b. *mezzo piano*

8. A rhythm that has sounds or silences where you do not normally expect them is called:

   a. a minor scale   b. *mezzo forte*   c. syncopation

BILLY THE KID

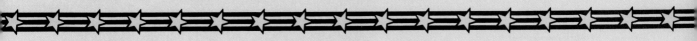

 "Street in a Frontier Town," from *Billy the Kid* by Aaron Copland

● Listen to this music. You will probably recognize some of the melodies. This is the way the music is organized.

Introduction

Part One
"Great Grand-dad"
"Git Along, Little Dogies"
"Old Chisholm Trail"

Part Two
"Jarabe"
"Good-Bye, Old Paint"

The Story
Billy the Kid is a ballet about the life of an outlaw. Billy's real name was William Bonney. In 1871, when he was twelve years old, he moved to New Mexico with his mother.

"Street in a Frontier Town" is one of the first scenes in *Billy the Kid*. The introduction suggests the vast, open prairie. Cowboys, the local sheriff, and other townspeople begin to appear and move about on the street.

Some Mexican dancers perform a *jarabe*, a traditional Mexican dance. Billy and his mother arrive on the scene. A fight breaks out between two of the cowboys. During the confusion, Billy's mother is accidentally killed. Her death turns Billy against everyone. He begins a career as an outlaw.

Billy

Mother

Sheriff

Once you are familiar with the music and the story that "Street in a Frontier Town" tells, you can act it out in mime and dance. **Mime** is silent drama. You can only use gestures, movement, and facial expressions to tell the story. You will need to learn to move silently.

• Plan your performance. Decide who will play each part. Here are all the characters.

Old Folks

Cowboys

Mexican Dancers

Tell the story clearly and simply through movement. Be sure that the audience can see the important things that happen. Practice until everyone knows how and when to move. You should move only when the music "tells" you to do so.

You may want to make scenery for your presentation. Large pictures of frontier buildings can be fastened to the wall behind you as a backdrop.

When you are ready to perform "Street in a Frontier Town," dress in costumes and invite your guests. Then share this music and the story of *Billy the Kid* with an audience.

UNIT 5 SOUNDS AND TEXTURES

THE PERCUSSION FAMILY

chimes

piano

timpani

xylophone

glockenspiel

celesta

String, brass, and woodwind instruments all look similar to the other members of their own families.

- Look at the instruments on these two pages. They are members of the **percussion** family. Do these instruments look similar to one another?
- Tell why you think these instruments belong to the same family.

Some percussion instruments can play definite pitches.

- Which percussion instruments on these pages are definite-pitched? Which are indefinite-pitched?
- Listen to the definite-pitched percussion instruments accompanying this **canon** (a song like a round).

Ding, Dong, the Bells Do Ring

From Music For Children, Vol. 1 by Carl Orff and Gunild Keetman

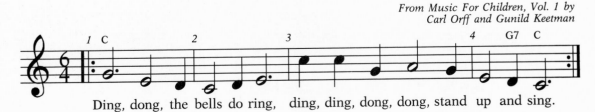

Ding, dong, the bells do ring,   ding, ding, dong, dong, stand up and sing.

The definite-pitched percussion instruments shown here are Orff (ôrf) instruments. They were developed by a German composer, Carl Orff. Some have bars of metal, some of wood. The instruments with metal bars (the glockenspiels and metallophones) are used in the accompaniment for "Ding, Dong, the Bells Do Ring."

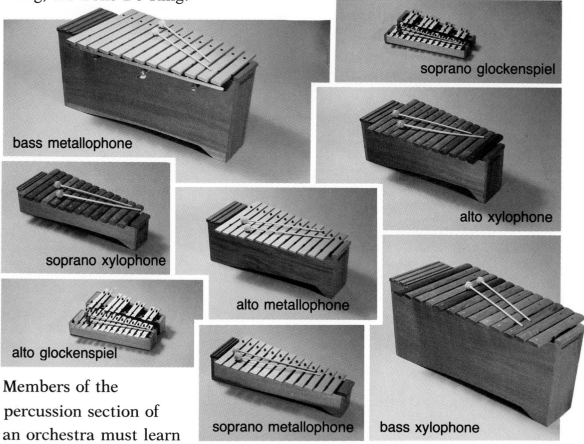

soprano glockenspiel

bass metallophone

alto xylophone

soprano xylophone

alto metallophone

alto glockenspiel

soprano metallophone

bass xylophone

Members of the percussion section of an orchestra must learn to perform on many different instruments. Part of the fun of seeing a symphony orchestra play is watching the percussion players move from instrument to instrument.

- Listen to some of the percussion instruments of the symphony orchestra. As you listen, identify as many instruments as you can.

 "Percussion Variations," from *Young Person's Guide to the Orchestra* by Benjamin Britten

This song was inspired by **ragtime,** a style of music popular in the 1890s. Ragtime was an early kind of jazz.

Winter's a Drag Rag

Words and music by Natalie Sleeth

Part I

I'm
1. tired ___ of the win - ter and I'm
2. tired ___ of the i - ci - cles and
3. but - ton up my jack - et and I

Part II

1. Oh, I am
2. _____
3. _____

sick to death of
leave be - hind the
but - ton up and

sick of all the snow,
all the heav-y clothes,
brave the sea-son's chill,

Dis-gust-ed with the cli-mate that would
I'm trou-bled by the temp-'ra-ture and
but of this aw-ful weath-er I have

all the snow! Some-how I feel just like an
heav - y clothes, the fall - ing temp - 'ra - ture and
face the chill! But of this weath - er I have

please an Es - ki - mo! I'd real - ly like to leave it but there's
wea - ry of its woes! I'd like to cure my fe - ver and to
tru - ly had my fill! I'm yearn - ing for a cro - cus or a

Es - ki - mo! I'd like to find a - noth - er
all its woes! I want to cure my cold and
had my fill, and I am yearn - ing for a

no-where else to go!
warm my numb-ing toes!
pret - ty daf - fo - dill!

I sure - ly hope that Spring is on the

place to go!
warm my toes!
daf - fo - dill!

I hope that Spring is on the

1.

way! 2. I'm

2.

way! I'd

way! 2. I'd like to

way! I'd like to

like to see a rob - in hop-ping cheer-ful-ly a-round! I'd

see the rob - ins all a-round,

love to find a mea-dow-lark and lis-ten to its sound! I

find a lark and lis-ten to its sound! I long to

long to watch the green-ing of the grass up-on the ground, but

watch the green - ing of the ground, but

I'm a-fraid it's true: the Spring is o - ver-due, and so I

Spring, it's true, is o - ver - due, and so I

3.

way, _____ I on - ly wish that it would come to-day!

way, _____ I wish that it would come to-day!

MUSIC TEXTURE: THICK AND THIN

When you sing or play a melody, you create a horizontal line of sound. It goes upward or downward according to the pitches in it. Melody alone has a thin texture.

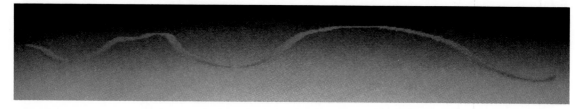

When you add instrumental accompaniment to the melody, you add layers of pitches (chords) along the path of the melody. This makes the texture thicker.

When you sing a round, the pitches in each part combine to create harmony.

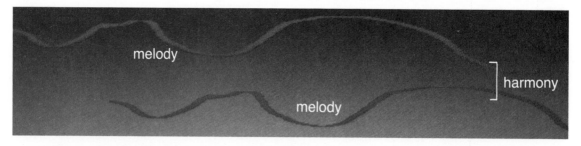

Combining different melodies also can create harmony.

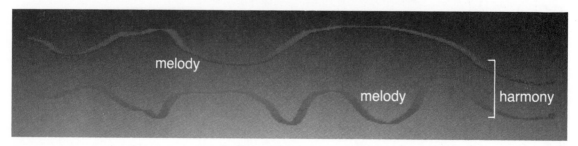

The more tones that sound at the same time, the thicker the texture becomes.

Music with indefinite pitch also has texture. A single line of rhythm has thin texture.

Combining lines of rhythm makes the texture thicker.

- Listen to *Toccata* for percussion instruments. Use hand movements to show when you hear changes in texture. Start with your palms together, one on top of the other. Pull your hands apart when you hear thick texture. Bring them back together when the texture is thin.

Toccata, Third Movement, by Carlos Chávez

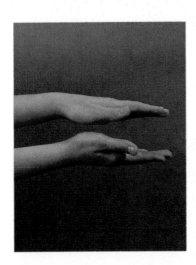
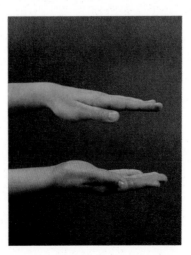
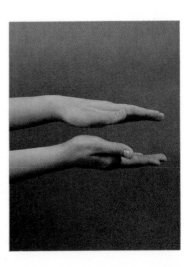

A PERCUSSION ACCOMPANIMENT

This song was written by elementary school students and
their music teacher in Memphis, Tennessee.

The Dream of Martin Luther King

Words and music by
Merle Gartrell and students
of Cummings Elementary School

1. Once there was a gen-tle-man ____ who talked a-bout a prom-ised land. __
2. In his dream he saw the peo-ple of this land __ walk-ing side by side. __

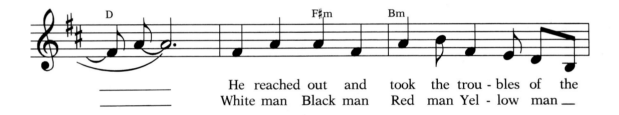

_____ He reached out and took the trou-bles of the
_____ White man Black man Red man Yel-low man __

peo-ple in his strong __ black hands. ____ He had a dream that
lov-ing one an-oth-er with pride. ____ Now he's __ gone a-

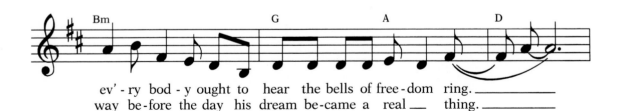

ev'-ry bod-y ought to hear the bells of free-dom ring. _____
way be-fore the day his dream be-came a real __ thing. _____

Now the peo-ple shout and sing a-bout the dream of Mar-tin Lu-ther King. __
But he'll hear the an-gels sing a-bout the dream of Mar-tin Lu-ther King. __

Sing a-bout the dream of Mar-tin Lu-ther King. —
Sing a-bout the dream of Mar-tin Lu-ther King. —

B Oh the dream — the dream of Mar-tin Lu-ther King. ——

Oh the dream —— the dream of Mar-tin Lu-ther King. _

— Sing a-bout the dream of Mar-tin Lu-ther King. —

C *4 times*

D.C. al Coda

He was, a man who loved peace, and he found, a faith and be-lief.
He preached, that vio-lence was wrong, and he knew, the fight would be long.
He talked, a-bout a new day, but he walked, a dan-ger-ous way.
He knew, the life of the slum, but he sang, *We Shall O-ver-come.*

⊕ *Coda Repeat and fade out*

— Sing a-bout the dream of Mar-tin Lu-ther King. —

- After you have learned the song, play this pattern throughout the A section. Use any definite-pitched percussion instrument.

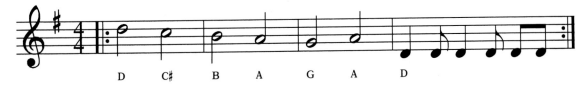

D   C♯   B   A   G   A   D

CREATING DIFFERENT TEXTURES

- Sing the melody (part 1) of "Great Day."
- Form two groups. Sing parts 1 and 2 together.

Great Day

Spiritual
Arranged by Jean Sinorr

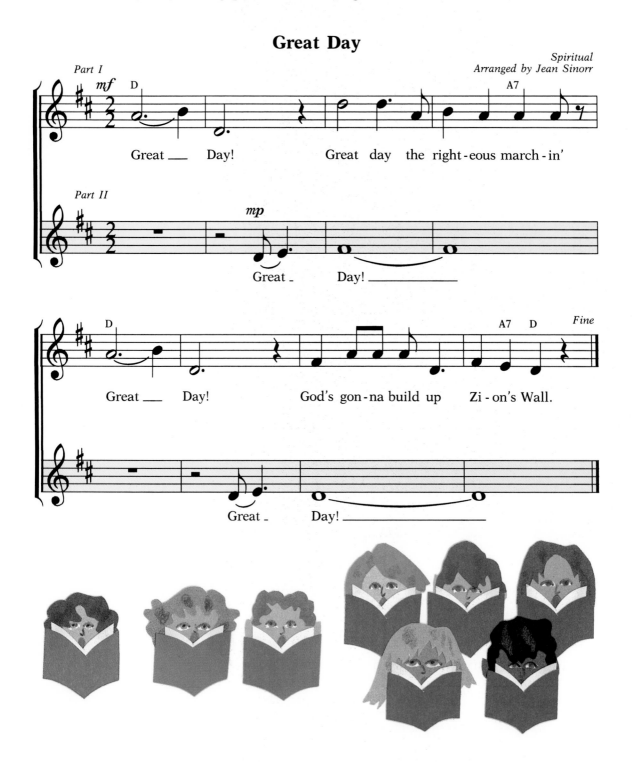

Part I

Great __ Day! Great day the right-eous march-in'

Part II

Great _ Day! ____

Great __ Day! God's gon-na build up Zi-on's Wall.

Great _ Day! ____

Char-iot road to the moun-tain top, God's gon-na build up Zi-on's Wall.

God's gon-na build up Zi-on's Wall.

D.C. al Fine

God he spoke and the char-iot stopped. God's gon-na build up Zi-on's Wall.

God's gon-na build up Zi-on's Wall.

Unison is several people singing or playing a single melody.

● Which creates thicker texture, singing in unison or in two parts?

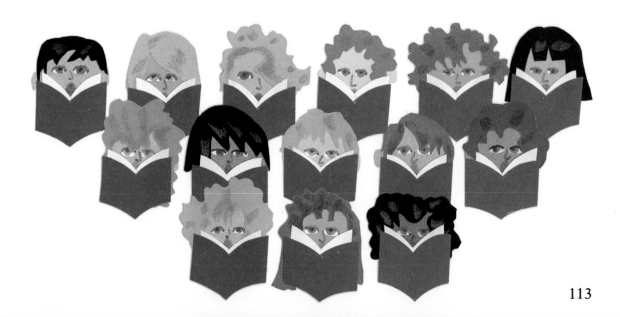

RONDO FORM

In **rondo** form, the A section returns after each different
section.

- Try saying the A section as you listen to "State Rondo."
  Then tell the form.

State Rondo

*Based on Rhythm Rondo by
Carl Orff and Gunild Keetman
Words by Shirley McRae*

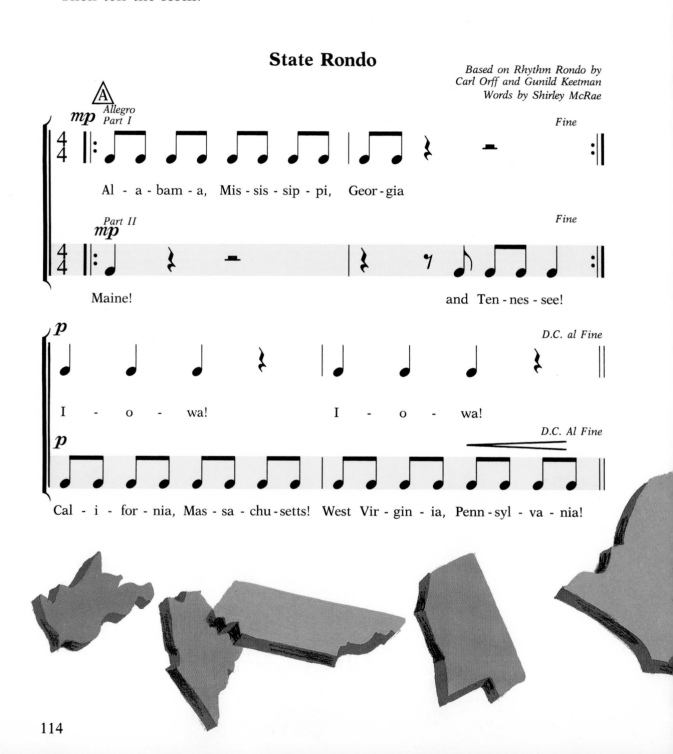

● Listen to another rondo. Decide how it is like "State Rondo."

 "Rondoapplause" by Carl Orff and Gunild Keetman

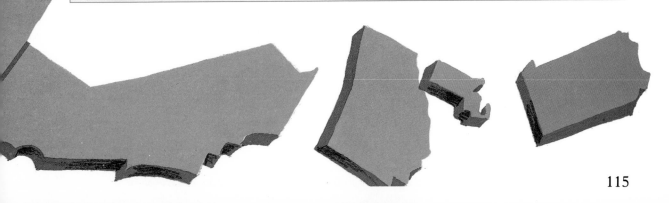

A troika is a vehicle pulled by three horses. Troikas were
used long ago in Russia.

Troika Speeding Through Russian Village by an unknown
painter of the nineteenth century

Troika Song

Music by Sergei Prokofiev
Words by Phyllis Stycos

We're rid - ing in a three horse sleigh to - day.

The snow is so spark - ling and bright!

In our three - horse sleigh we'll ride all through the day

And we'll ride half - way through the night.

From "Lieutenant Kije"

- Listen for "Troika Song" in this music. How many times do you hear it?

 "Troika," from *Lieutenant Kijé Suite* by Sergei Prokofiev

| AABB | ABBA | ABACABA | AAAA | ABACABCA |

- Which combination of letters above represents the form of "Troika"?
- Which represents the form of a more usual rondo?

SERGEI PROKOFIEV

Sergei Prokofiev (ser-gā′ prō-kof′yəf) was a Russian composer who lived from 1891 to 1953. His interest in creating music began before he could read or write. By the time he was nine he had composed an opera. He composed a symphony when he was twelve. When he was eighteen he won prizes for composition and piano playing.

Prokofiev wrote music for ballets and films and also adapted this music for the concert hall. *Lieutenant Kijé* is one piece written for a film. Another of Prokofiev's compositions you may recognize is *Peter and the Wolf*. It is an orchestral fairy tale written for young people.

CREATE A WINTER RONDO

- Create your own rondo. Use this song as the A section in your composition.

The Breath of Winter

Words and music by Laura Koulish

The breath of win-ter fills the air, _ it jells in - to an ic - y stare, _

And with the whirl-ing, swirl-ing snow The sounds of _ win - ter _ come and go.

- Divide into five groups. Each group will create one of the sections in the rondo.

Each group should choose one of the five senses (sight, hearing, touch, smell, taste) to write about. Use the exercise on the next page to get your group started.

Use each member's ideas to create the group's section of the rondo. Include an accompaniment on percussion instruments. Consider dynamic levels, tempo, and movement. Finally, decide who will perform the group's section of the rondo.

- Complete one of the following thoughts. Share your ideas with the others in your group.

> Winter looks like. . .
>
> Winter sounds like. . .
>
> Winter feels like. . .
>
> Winter smells like. . .
>
> Winter tastes like. . .

This illustration shows how sections are combined to form a rondo.

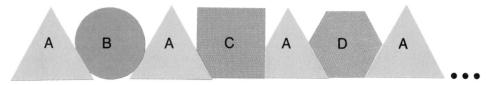

- Listen to each group's composition. Decide the order of each composition in your rondo. Label each using the letters B, C, D, E, and F to show the order.
- Perform your rondo using "The Breath of Winter" as the A section.

WEAVING RHYTHMS AND HARMONY

● Use body percussions as you say the words.

Winter Rhythms

Finger Snap:
Clap:
Pat Legs:
Stamp:

L   R
Let's   go   ski! (It's cold!)

Winter in Union Square, Childe Hassam, METROPOLITAN MUSEUM OF ART, New York.

Artists use texture to help them express their ideas. In this painting, *Union Square,* by Childe Hassam (has′əm) a short brush stroke is used to create the desired effect.

• Follow the rhythm pattern as you say this chant.

Ice and Sleet

*Based on a rhythm example in
"Music For Children," Vol. 1 by
Carl Orff and Gunild Keetman
Words by M.D.*

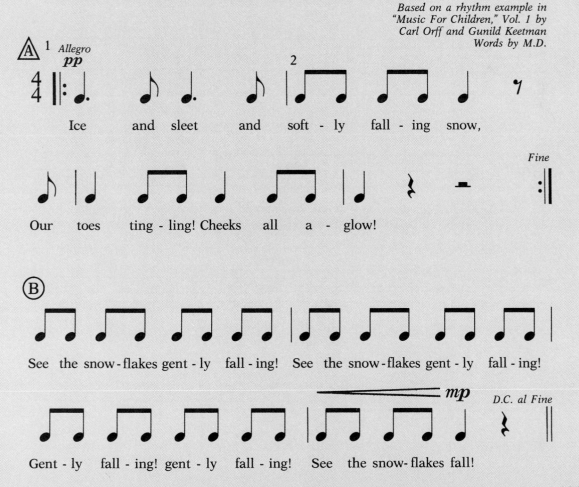

A ¹ *Allegro*
pp

Ice   and   sleet   and   soft - ly   fall - ing   snow,

Our   toes   ting - ling! Cheeks   all   a - glow!

B

See the snow-flakes gent - ly   fall - ing! See the snow-flakes gent - ly   fall - ing!

mp   *D.C. al Fine*

Gent - ly   fall - ing! gent - ly   fall - ing! See the snow-flakes fall!

- Learn both parts of this song. Then combine the parts to create harmony.

Harmony

Words and music by Artie Kaplan and Norman J. Simon

1. The time has come, let us be-gin _ With all our voic-es
2. Like the shep-herd guards his sheep, _ Watch your child-ren

join-ing in, ___ To sing of love and broth-er-hood, _
as they sleep, _ And like the pot-ter turns his clay, _

And peo-ple do-ing what they should To help their fel-low
Help us shape a bet-ter day, ___ Let us sing a

man be free, _ And fill this land with har-mo-ny, ___
song of love, _ For there's one thing I'm cer-tain of, ___

The young, the old the rich, the poor, _ Mak-ing sounds _
Love will fill the hearts of men, _ And peace will come on

122

Refrain

Descant

nev - er heard be - fore. _____ La la la la la
earth ___ once a - gain. _____ La la la la la

Melody

nev - er heard be - fore. _____ La la la la la
earth ___ once a - gain. _____ La la la la la

Har - mo - ny, ___ har - mo - ny, ___ Let's all join in

Har - mo - ny, ___ har - mo - ny, ___ Let's all join in

har - mo - ny, ___ And sing a - way ___ the hurt and fear, ___ A

har - mo - ny, ___ And sing a - way ___ the hurt and fear, ___ A

Great new day will soon be here. _____

Great new day will soon ___ be ___ here. _____

RHYTHM PATTERNS
IN A CREOLE SONG

During the 1800s, people selling food on the streets of New Orleans often sang to attract customers. "Baked Potato" was a familiar song in the French Quarter. It has rhythms that give it a special excitement.

The main rhythm pattern uses dotted quarter notes (♩.).

● Say these rhythm patterns:

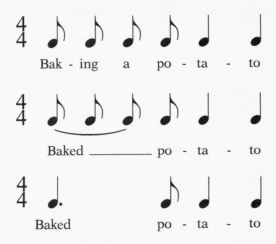

The dotted quarter note sounds as long as three eighth notes (♪♪♪).

● Find this rhythm pattern in the song:

Baked Potato

Creole Folk Song
Words Adapted

1. Come and get your baked po - ta - to,
2. Add some but - ter, salt and pep - per,

baked po - ta - to, baked po - ta - to.
salt and pep - per, salt and pep - per.

Come and get your baked po - ta - to,
Add some but - ter, salt and pep - per,

Care - ful, it may be hot!
Care - ful, it may be hot!

LOUIS MOREAU GOTTSCHALK

Louis Moreau Gottschalk (loo′is mô-rō′ got′shôk) was born in 1829 in New Orleans. He was one of the first American composers to become well known outside the United States.

When he was a boy, he listened to minstrel shows near his home. Years later he used a favorite folk melody from these shows in a piano composition, "Bamboula." Gottschalk died in 1869.

Hershy Kay, an American composer, used "Bamboula" for a ballet based on Gottschalk's music. The ballet is called *Cakewalk*. In it, "Bamboula" is known as "Grand Walkaround."

- Listen for the familiar folk song in "Grand Walkaround."

 "Grand Walkaround," from *Cakewalk* by Louis Moreau Gottschalk and Hershy Kay

LISTENING FOR DIFFERENT METERS

Meter in music refers to how beats are grouped.

- Pat the strong beat as you listen to this music. Identify the meter of each part as either $\frac{3}{4}$ or $\frac{4}{4}$.

 "Xylophone Invention" by Carl Orff and Gunild Keetman

- Remember that when beats are grouped in threes, two weaker beats follow every strong beat. Say this chant in $\frac{3}{4}$ meter.

Winter Thunderstorm Chant

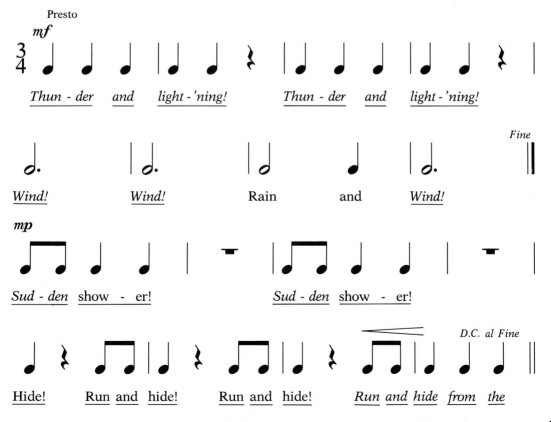

127

SINGING A SONG IN $\frac{3}{4}$ METER

● Listen to this song. Pat the strong beat.

Sweet Betsy from Pike

Folk Tune
Adapted by M.S.

2. 'Twas early one evening they camped on the Platte,
   By the side of the road on a shady green flat.
   Sweet Betsy, sore footed, lay down in repose,
   While Ike kept the watch o'er his Pike County rose.

3. They soon reached the desert where Betsy gave out,
   And down in the sand she lay rollin' about.
   When Ike saw sweet Betsy he said with surprise,
   "You'd better get up, you'll get sand in your eyes."

4. Said Ike, "Ole Pike County, I'll go back to you."
   Said Betsy, "You'll go by yourself if you do,
   There's no time for pleasure and no time for rest,
   In spite of our troubles we'll keep headin' west."

5. They camped on the prairie for weeks upon weeks.
   They swam the wide rivers and crossed the tall peaks,
   And soon they were rollin' in nuggets of gold.
   You may not believe it but that's what we're told.

TAKE ANOTHER LOOK

Sounds and Textures

Every stage in the history of our country has been different. Events, decisions, and thoughts have given each period its own special qualities. Every piece of music also has its own special character.

Musical lines heard at the same time can create a variety of harmonies and textures. (Sing "Ding, Dong, the Bells Do Ring," and "Winter Is a Drag Rag.")

Patterns of rhythm and melody can be put together and make the simplest music interesting. (Perform "State Rondo," then "Baked Potato.")

The tone quality of instruments affects the music. (Perform "Troika," then "Ice and Sleet.")

Music can even change the way people think, feel, and act. (Sing "Harmony.")

Learning about ways that some of the musical elements are used helps us to better understand the music of our country and the important effect that music has had on the American people.

JUST CHECKING

1. Which are percussion instruments?

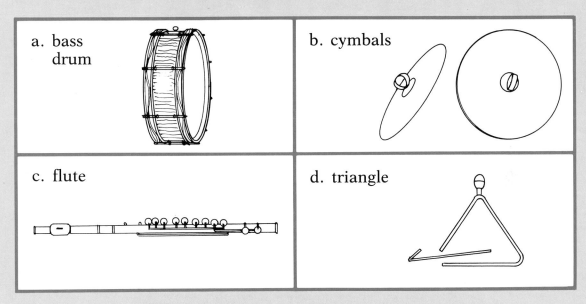

a. bass drum

b. cymbals

c. flute

d. triangle

2. Which group of eighth notes is as long as the dotted quarter note (𝅘𝅥𝅭)?

a. 𝅘𝅥𝅮 𝅘𝅥𝅮   b. 𝅘𝅥𝅮𝅘𝅥𝅮   c. 𝅘𝅥𝅮 𝅘𝅥𝅮 𝅘𝅥𝅮

3. Which best illustrates thick texture?

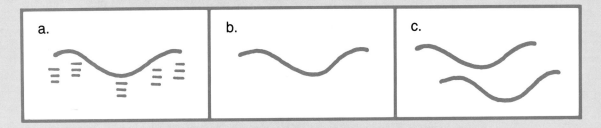

a.

b.

c.

4. Which combination of letters shows the plan of a rondo form?

a. AAA   b. ABACA   c. AABB

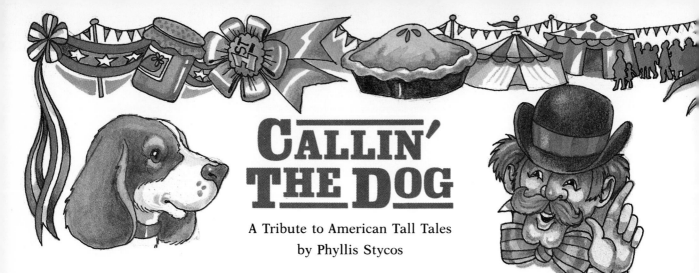

CALLIN' THE DOG

A Tribute to American Tall Tales
by Phyllis Stycos

This is the story of a guy named Willie and a contest at an old-fashioned county fair in the Midwest. It takes place about 1901 in Brown County. There, one of the favorite pastimes was telling stories, especially "tall tales"—stories that stretched the truth a lot in funny and entertaining ways.

People even had tall-tale competitions. They were called "Callin' the Dog" contests because the winner won a fine dog and got to call the dog home.

● Sing "The Brown County Fair."

The Brown County Fair

Words and music by Phyllis C. Stycos

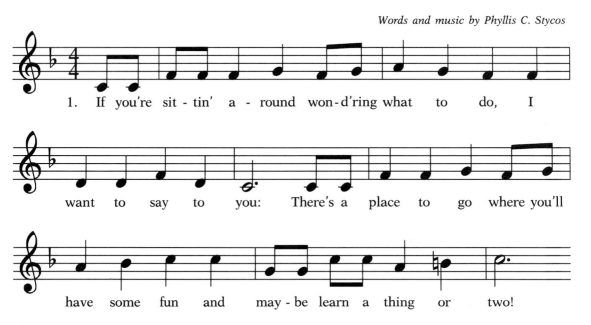

1. If you're sit-tin' a-round won-d'ring what to do, I want to say to you: There's a place to go where you'll have some fun and may-be learn a thing or two!

The Brown Coun-ty Fair hap-pens once a year and
we can hard-ly wait to see all the sights and the
col-ored lights as we walk through that gate!

Refrain

The Brown Coun-ty Fair is the big-gest and best! It's a
great coun-ty fair, that's true! The Brown Coun-ty Fair can
beat them all! It's there for me and you!

2. You should see the tents,
They're a hundred yards tall.
And the flagpoles reach the sky!
Our dairy cows give us only cream.
Our horses are twenty hands high.

The wonderful cakes that the ladies bake,
Are heaven to a hungry man.
They bake 'em tall and they're so light,
They float right out of the pan.
Refrain

3. Come right on over to the poultry tent,
You'll have a lot of fun.
The chickens we show are as big as a mule,
And each egg weighs a ton.

The merry-go-round takes an hour or two,
Just going once around.
And the Ferris wheel takes longer than that,
To get you back to the ground.
Refrain

One day at the fair, there was a contest to see who could tell the tallest tale. The prize was a beautiful hound-dog puppy.

Word about the contest spread around town. Soon many people gathered to enter the contest or just to listen and enjoy the tales. John, the blacksmith, told the first story. He had a strange and funny tale to tell.

● Sing "Fooba Wooba John."

Fooba Wooba John

American Folk Song

1. Saw a flea kick a tree,
2. Saw a crow fly - in' low,
3. Saw a whale chase a snail,
4. Saw a louse push a mouse,

Foo - ba, woo - ba, foo - ba, woo - ba

Saw a flea kick a tree,
Saw a crow fly - in' low,
Saw a whale chase a snail,
Saw a louse push a mouse,

Foo - ba, woo - ba, John!

Saw a flea kick a tree in the mid - dle of the sea!
Saw a crow fly - in' low sev - 'ral miles be - neath the snow!
Saw a whale chase a snail all a - round a wa - ter pail!
Saw a louse push a mouse down the chim - ney through the house!

Whoa, John, Oh, John, Foo - ba, woo - ba, John.

Lillian, the town librarian, was next to enter the contest. She mentioned how intelligent librarians were and said that she wanted to share some of her experiences.

● Sing "The Historian."

The Historian

American Folk Song

1. I was born a hun-dred thou-sand years a-go, _____
2. I was there when No-ah built his fa-mous Ark, _____
3. If you don't be-lieve that what I say is true, _____

And there's not a thing in his-t'ry I don't know. _____
And I crawled in through the win-dow af-ter dark. _____
Then what dif-f'rence does it real-ly make to you? _____

I saw Pe-ter, Paul and Mo-ses play-ing "Ring a-round the Ro-ses,"
I saw Jo-nah eat the whale and Dan-iel twist the li-on's tail; ___
I'm just shoot-in' you this line ___ for to pass a-way the time; ___

I can lick the guy who says it is-n't so. _____
and I crossed the land of Ca-naan on a lark. _____
and so now I'm goin' to quit be-cause I'm through. ___

Then came Matthew, the town clerk.
He said he hadn't had an
adventuresome life but he knew
someone who had.

● Sing "Old Joe Clark."

Old Joe Clark

Refrain

American Folk Song

'Round and 'round, Old Joe Clark, 'Round and 'round I say;

'Round and 'round, Old Joe Clark, I have-n't long to stay.

Verse

1. Old Joe Clark, he had a house Six-teen stor-ies high:
2. I went down to old Joe's house, Nev-er been there be-fore;

D.C. al Fine

Ev-'ry sto-ry in that house was full of chick-en pie.
He slept on the feath-er bed And I slept on the floor.

A woman named Nellie was in the crowd with several of her friends. They said, "There have been so many stories about what men have done. We want to enter this contest to tell about what Annie Christmas did."

● Sing "Annie Christmas."

Annie Christmas

Words and music by Phyllis C. Stycos

1. Let me tell you 'bout a wom-an who was six feet tall. __
2. Oh, the win-ter days went slow-ly and they saw no sails, __
3. Then the sun went down and ev-'ry-bod-y passed the news __

Big __ An-nie was her name. She was a friend to all. __
But on Christ-mas Eve the ship ar-rived thru wind and gales! __
Our __ An-nie was a-run-nin' hard thru Ba-ton Rouge. __

She pi-lot-ed a flat-boat on the Mis-sis-sip-pi run.
They load-ed up the flat-boat and they piled it up with toys.
She gal-loped through the dark-ness pull-in' on the pre-cious load.

At three __ hun-dred pounds __ ev-'ry ar-gu-ment she won!
Said An-nie, "Give the rope to me and cast her off, my boys!"
Her feet and hands were go-in' strong. She's burn-in' up the road!

138

An - nie wait - ed in New Or - leans ma - ny days. __
An - nie took the rope and pulled with all her might. _
An - nie got to Nat - chez at the dawn of day. __

A clip - per ship from France was cut - tin' thru the waves. _
The boat was start - in' slow; she pulled the rope up tight. _
A crowd of peo - ple met her and she heard them say, __

It was load - ed up with toys the go - in' it was rough!
Then her steps be - gan to quick - en; she broke in - to a run.
"Chil - dren wak - ing up for Christ - mas will see these love - ly toys.

They're all __ due for Christ - mas up at Nat - chez on the bluff.
The boat be - gan to skip the waves and Anne was hav - in' fun! _
We love you, An - nie Christ - mas; so will all the girls and boys!"

Refrain

An - nie Christ - mas was a great old gal. _ She was ev - 'ry - bod - y's

friend and pal! _ She went up the Mis - sis - sip - pi with the toys _

(1.,2.) Will she get there in time to bring some Christ - mas joy? __
(3.) And she got there in time to bring some Christ - mas joys! __

139

The Elliott family entered as a group. Each person had part of a story to tell. It was about Pecos Bill and his horse, Widowmaker.

● Sing "Pecos Bill."

Pecos Bill

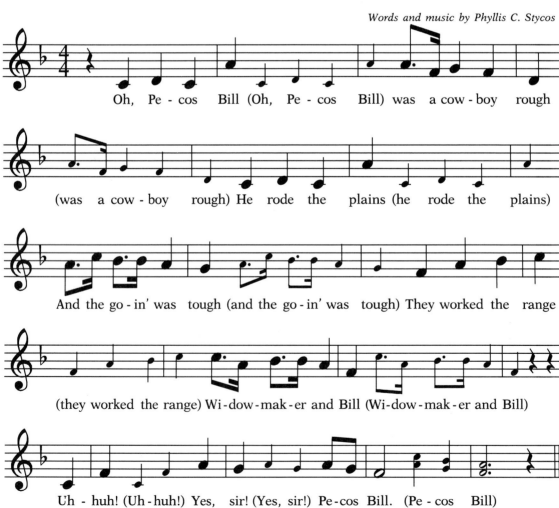

Words and music by Phyllis C. Stycos

Oh, Pe-cos Bill (Oh, Pe-cos Bill) was a cow-boy rough

(was a cow-boy rough) He rode the plains (he rode the plains)

And the go-in' was tough (and the go-in' was tough) They worked the range

(they worked the range) Wi-dow-mak-er and Bill (Wi-dow-mak-er and Bill)

Uh-huh! (Uh-huh!) Yes, sir! (Yes, sir!) Pe-cos Bill. (Pe-cos Bill)

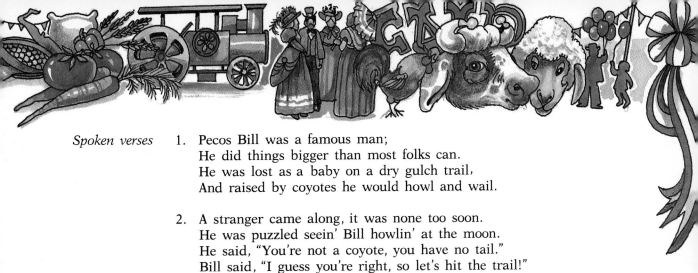

Spoken verses

1. Pecos Bill was a famous man;
   He did things bigger than most folks can.
   He was lost as a baby on a dry gulch trail,
   And raised by coyotes he would howl and wail.

2. A stranger came along, it was none too soon.
   He was puzzled seein' Bill howlin' at the moon.
   He said, "You're not a coyote, you have no tail."
   Bill said, "I guess you're right, so let's hit the trail!"

3. Bill needed a horse so he raised a colt.
   He taught Widowmaker how to buck and bolt.
   He fed him dynamite and glyc'rin, too.
   Wasn't anything Bill and his horse couldn't do!

4. Bill roped a herd of cattle with a rattlesnake.
   When he rode Widowmaker the earth would shake.
   He dug the Rio Grande, as ev'ryone knows,
   And he kept real busy puttin' horns on toads.

5. He rode a tornado on the Oklahoma track.
   Bill eared it down, then he climbed on its back.
   It threw him left and it threw him right.
   He rode that thing 'til it gave up the fight.

After the Elliotts had finished their song, no one else came forward to enter the contest. Davy, the barber, asked Willie, "Are you joining our contest?" Everyone knew what a great storyteller Willie was. Nobody could outdo Willie.

Willie looked surprised and said, "Why, how could I? I've never stretched the truth in my whole life." Davy said, "That does it, Willie. With that statement, you have told the tallest tale of all. You've got to be today's winner. You can call this dog home with you tonight."

Willie pretended to look puzzled about why he had won. Then he said, "I wanted to win the contest and I'm glad I did. But, there are some folks here who probably want this dog even more than I do. So I'd like them to have it." With that, he gave the dog to the Elliott family, and everyone agreed that this had been the best Brown County fair ever.

UNIT **6** AMERICAN MUSIC ON PARADE

The Civil War threatened to split the United States in the early 1860s. Songs from this period celebrated victories or mourned defeats. The songs told of patriotism and hope for freedom. Other songs were for pure enjoyment.

"Civil War Medley"

A SONG FROM LONG AGO

During the Civil War, the soldiers often ate peanuts, which they called goober peas.

● Sing the melody first; then sing the harmony. When the two parts are combined, the harmony should be a little softer than the melody.

Goober Peas

Civil War Marching Song

Harmony: Yum, Yum, Yum, _____ Yu - um, Yum, Yum, Yum,

Melody:
1. Sit - ting by the road - side _____ on a sum - mer day, _____
2. Just be - fore the bat - tle, _ the Gen - 'ral hears a row, _____ He
3. Now our song has las - ted _____ al - most long e - nough, _____ The

Harmony: Yum, Yum, Yum, _____ Yu - um, Yum, Yum, Yum,

Chat - ting with my mess - mates _ pass - ing time a - way. _____
says, "The Yanks are com - ing; _ I hear their ri - fles now!" _____ He
sub - ject's in - ter - est - ing, _ but rhymes are might - y rough. _____

Yum, Yum, Yum, _____ Yu - um, Yum, Yum, Yum,

Dynamic markings tell how loud or soft the music should be.

● What are the dynamic markings in "Goober Peas"? Which is the loudest?

145

F O C U S   O N

Burl Ives

Songs from all periods of American history are still sung today. One musician who has helped to keep these songs popular is Burl Ives.

Burl Ives was born in 1915 in Illinois. At the age of four he started singing at church services. He began his career in the 1930s as a ballad singer. With his guitar and his unusual voice, he became a leading folk singer.

Ives became a top recording artist and went on to a career in radio, nightclubs, and concerts. He starred in thirteen Broadway shows, many movies, and a television series.

Ives has received four honorary doctorate degrees and many awards. In 1975, he won his native state's highest award, the Lincoln Lauriette Award. His songs praise our heritage and remind us that this is our land and that we must protect it.

 "Leather-Winged Bat," performed by Burl Ives

A familiar melody is used in "Battle Hymn," a composition
for band. The melody is played by different instruments and
with other melodies at the same time. One part of the
melody is also heard as a **canon.** In a canon, the melody
repeats as it does in a round.

"Battle Hymn" has a *coda* (kōd′ə). A **coda** is a concluding
section of a piece of music.

● Decide what dynamic markings might be used for the
  different parts of this piece. Choose from these markings:

$$pp \quad p \quad mp \quad mf \quad f \quad ff$$

● What happens at the very end of this piece?

 "Battle Hymn" by Morton Gould

This Civil War song is still very popular today.

● Follow the dynamic markings as you sing this song.

Battle Hymn of the Republic

Music by William Steffe
Words by Julia Ward Howe

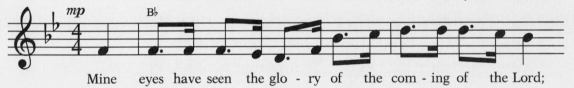

Mine eyes have seen the glo - ry of the com - ing of the Lord;

He is tram - pling out the vin - tage where the grapes of wrath are stored;

He has loosed the fate - ful light - ning of his ter - ri - ble swift sword;

His truth is march - ing on.

Refrain

Glo-ry, Glo-ry, Hal-le-lu - jah! Glo-ry, Glo-ry, Hal-le-lu - jah!

Glo - ry, Glo - ry! Glo - ry, Glo - ry!

Glo-ry, Glo-ry, Hal-le-lu - jah! His truth is march-ing on.

Glo - ry, Glo - ry! His truth is march-ing on.

BAND OR ORCHESTRA?

An orchestra includes members who play all four families of instruments: the strings, the woodwinds, the brasses, and the percussions. The modern symphony orchestra has about 100 members. Over half of them play string instruments. Only a few woodwinds and brasses are in the orchestra, but each adds a special tone color. In the percussion section, two or three people play all the instruments.

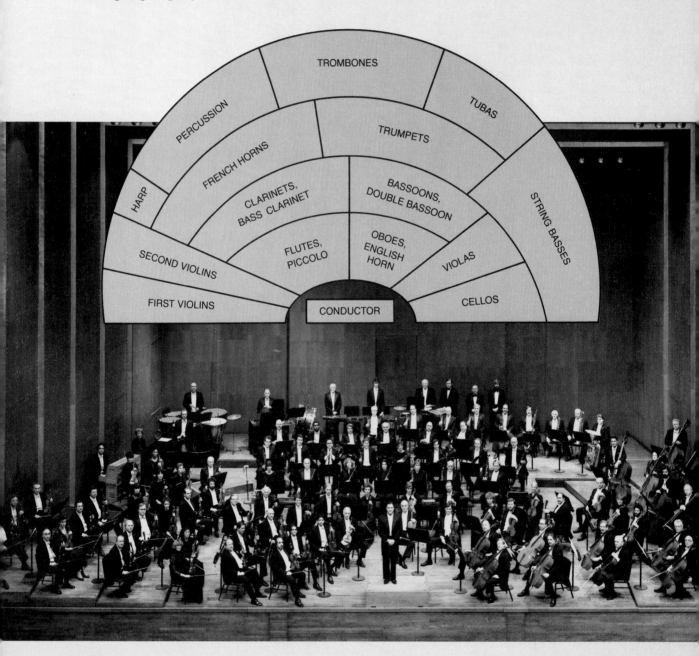

A **concert band** (also called a **symphonic band**) includes members who play only three families of instruments: woodwinds, brasses, and percussions. Each of these sections is larger than it is in an orchestra. Since bands were originally marching groups, string instruments are not used. The concert band has about the same number of members as an orchestra.

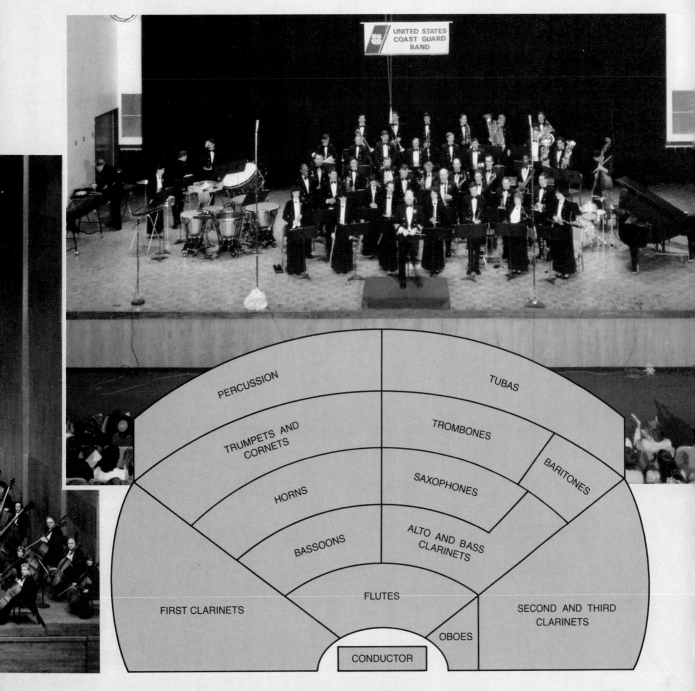

UNITED STATES
COAST GUARD
BAND

PERCUSSION

TUBAS

TRUMPETS AND
CORNETS

TROMBONES

HORNS

SAXOPHONES

BARITONES

BASSOONS

ALTO AND BASS
CLARINETS

FIRST CLARINETS

FLUTES

SECOND AND THIRD
CLARINETS

OBOES

CONDUCTOR

Another familiar band is the **marching band.** Like the concert band, it has no string instruments. Members of a marching band must be able to march at the same time they play their instruments. Precision marching routines are usually part of a school or college marching band performance.

- Read this poem in a way that shows the excitement of a marching band.

Ten Tom-Toms

Ten tom-toms, timpani, too!
Ten tall tubas and an old kazoo!
Ten trombones! Give them a hand!
The sitting, standing, running, marching,
Big brass band!

—*Anonymous*

● What band instruments are mentioned in this song from the hit Broadway musical "Barnum"?

Come Follow the Band

Words and music by
Cy Coleman and Michael Stewart

mp

Come fol-low the band. ___ Where-ev-er it's at, ___

Let both of your feet ___ beat time to the drum ___ and feel your

heart go rat - a - tat - tat. ___ A flag in your hand, ___

a plume in your hat. ___ Bat - tal-lions of brass ___ pass and

catch the light. ___ Is there a sight that's sweet - er than that? ___

See the pret-ty la-dy toss that ba-ton high,

Ain't she cute as a dai-sy? Watch the fel-la with the

big bass drum go by. Ain't you glad that you stayed?

Hear the tu-ba play that oom-pah-pah, oh my, ain't it driv-in' you

cra-zy? Don't you be so darn la-zy,

___ Bet-ter hur-ry and join that big pa-rade. ___ Up out-a your seat, ___ down off-a the stand. ___ Step out to the sweet ___ beat the bu-gle plays. _ A sound that you'll re-mem-ber all your days. _ And when you see the lead-er proud-ly raise _ his hand ___ ___ just fol-low the band. ___

A FAVORITE SONG OF ABRAHAM LINCOLN

Abraham Lincoln made many speeches, and he always seemed to have a funny story to tell. At an early age, he discovered that he could make people think more clearly if he made them laugh first. He loved music, especially this funny song.

- Look for the *fermata* (⌢) over some of the notes in "Blue Tail Fly." Make any note over which the *fermata* is placed a little longer.
- As you listen to this song, pat the strong beats and clap the others. How many beats are in each measure?

Blue Tail Fly

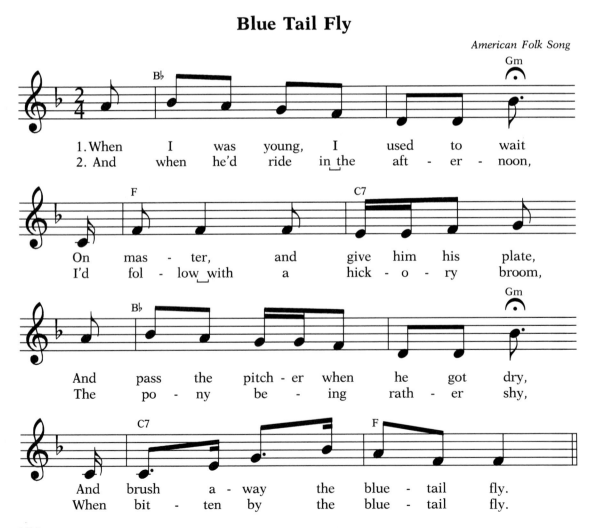

American Folk Song

1. When I was young, I used to wait
2. And when he'd ride in the aft - er - noon,

On mas - ter, and give him his plate,
I'd fol - low with a hick - o - ry broom,

And pass the pitch - er when he got dry,
The po - ny be - ing rath - er shy,

And brush a - way the blue - tail fly.
When bit - ten by the blue - tail fly.

Refrain

F

Jim - mie crack corn and I don't care,

C7

Jim - mie crack corn and I don't care,

F

Jim - mie crack corn and I don't care,

My mas - ter's gone a - way.

3. One day he rode around the farm;
   The flies so numerous they did swarm;
   One chanced to bite him on the thigh,
   He switched away the blue-tail fly!

4. The pony run, he jump, he pitch,
   He threw my master in the ditch.
   He died, and the jury wondered why—
   The verdict was, "The blue-tail fly!"

5. They laid him under a 'simmon tree;
   His epitaph is there to see;
   "Beneath this stone I'm forced to lie,
   A victim of the blue-tail fly."

- Listen to this song. How many beats are in each measure?

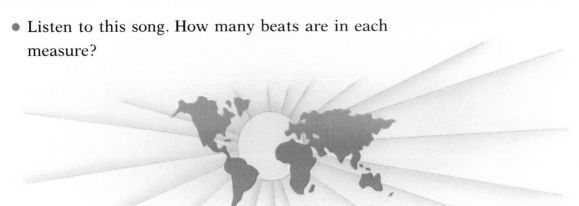

Sun Don't Set in the Morning

Southern Folk Hymn

Refrain

Sun don't set in the morn - in',

Sun don't set in the morn - in', Lord,

Sun don't set in the morn - in';

Light shines 'round the world.

Verse

Pray on, _____ pray - in' sis - ter, Pray on, _____ pray - in' sis - ter,
broth - er, broth - er,

Pray on, _____ pray - in' sis - ter, Light shines 'round the world.
broth - er,

Spirituals are just what the name suggests—songs that have a religious or spiritual meaning. Spirituals are the creation of black Americans and are one of their gifts to the world of music.

Interest in spirituals grew during the early part of the nineteenth century. Credit for introducing them to the American public and the world belongs to Fisk University in Nashville, Tennessee. The Fisk Jubilee Singers toured the United States in 1871 and were so successful that they also toured Europe.

Choirs and choruses today still enjoy singing spirituals.

Below, a portrait of the original Jubilee Singers in Queen Victoria's Court, by Edmund Havel. At right, today's Fisk Jubilee Singers standing in front of the portrait.

A MUSICAL MAP

This song is a musical map. The "drinking gourd" is the Big Dipper, a constellation found in the northern sky. Black people escaping from slavery followed the drinking gourd to find the North—and freedom.

Follow the Drinkin' Gourd

Black American Spiritual
Adapted by Paul Campbell

1. When the sun comes back and the first quail calls, _____ Fol - low _____ the Drink - in' Gourd. _____ Then the Old Man is a - wait - in' for to car - ry you to free - dom, _____ Fol - low the Drink - in' Gourd.

2. Now the riv-er bank-'ll make _____ a might-y good road; _____ The dead trees - 'll show you the way. And the left _____ foot, _____ peg - foot, _____ trav - el - in' _____ on, Just you fol - low the Drink - in' Gourd.

3. Now the riv - er ends _____ be - tween two hills; _____ Fol - low _____ the Drink - in' Gourd. _____ And _____ there's an - oth - er riv - er on the oth - er _____ side, Just you fol - low the Drink - in' Gourd.

Refrain

Fol - low _____ the Drink - in' Gourd, _

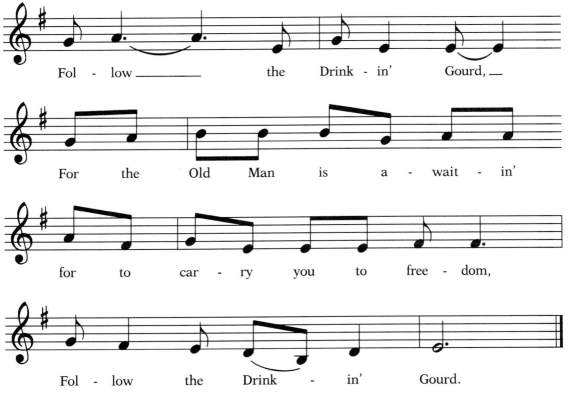

Fol - low _____ the Drink - in' Gourd, _____

For the Old Man is a - wait - in'

for to car - ry you to free - dom,

Fol - low the Drink - in' Gourd.

WILLIAM GRANT STILL

William Grant Still (1895–1978) was born in Woodville, Mississippi. In 1936 he led the Los Angeles Philharmonic at the Hollywood Bowl. This made him the first black to conduct a major symphony orchestra. Still is also well known as a composer. "Festive Overture" won first prize in a composition contest.

- Listen for major and minor sections in the first half of "Festive Overture."

 "Festive Overture" by William Grant Still

A RHYTHMIC TONGUE TWISTER

● Listen for the very short sounds in this tongue twister.

Madalina Catalina

Camp Song

Mad - a - li - na Cat - a - li - na Whoop - a - stin - a Wil - a - mi - na

Oop - sy Doop - sy Woop - sy was her name. name.

1. She had two eyes that were in her head,

one was yel - low and the oth - er was red.

2. She had two teeth in her mouth,

one point - ed east and the oth - er point - ed south.

● Clap the rhythm and count the beat as you sing the refrain
for "Madalina Catalina."

162

- Find the beats that contain four equal sounds. Say the word or words that go with each of these beats.
- Look at the song and see how these four sounds are notated.

Four of these notes sound as long as a quarter note.
Each one is called a **sixteenth note.**

 This is a sixteenth note.	Four sixteenth notes have a double beam.	A **sixteenth rest** lasts as long as a sixteenth note.

Sixteenth and eighth notes can be combined in different ways to sound for one beat.

- Find the beats that contain combinations of eighth and sixteenth notes in "Madalina Catalina." Say the words that go with them.

Concert bands were originally formed to provide music for outdoor events. The first American concert bands appeared after the Civil War. One well-known band toured the country and performed songs that became popular during the war. It wasn't until 1918, after World War I, that concert bands reached their peak in popularity. The United States Marine Band is considered one of the world's best-known concert bands. John Philip Sousa was the leader of the United States Marine Band from 1880–1892 and was responsible for making it the fine band that it is today.

- Locate the different families of instruments. Which family is missing from a concert band?

John Philip Sousa's Concert Band

JOHN PHILIP SOUSA

John Philip Sousa (soo′zə) was an American composer who lived from 1854 to 1932. After a successful career as the leader of the U.S. Marine Corps band, he formed his own band. Sousa wrote operettas, orchestral suites, and many songs. He is most famous for the almost 100 lively marches he wrote. Among them is "The Stars and Stripes Forever." Sousa once said that "a march should make a man with a wooden leg step out." The beat of his marches may do just that.

- This is one of the most famous marches ever written. Listen for sixteenth notes.

 "The Stars and Stripes Forever" by John Philip Sousa

A **drum cadence** is a pattern used to accompany marching. It is usually sixteen beats long.

- Create a drum cadence by patting the rhythm as you say "Ten Tom-Toms."

Ten tom - toms, tim - pa - ni, too!

Ten tall tu - bas and an old ka - zoo!

Ten trom - bones! Give them a hand! The

sit - ting, stand - ing, run - ning, march - ing big brass band!

Here are the dynamic markings in order from softest to loudest.

$$pp \quad p \quad mp \quad mf \quad f \quad ff$$

- Decide how to use different dynamic levels to make your drum cadence more interesting.

FORM IN AMERICAN MARCHES

Most marches have a similar basic form. The march begins
with a brief introduction. It is followed by two short,
melodically contrasting sections, often called simply the **first**
and **second strains.** The third part is usually more singable
and is called the **trio.** After a brief interlude, known as the
break strain, the trio is repeated.

The usual sections
of a march are:

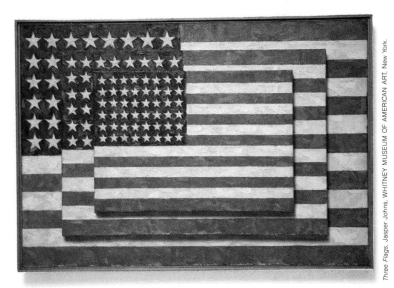

Introduction First Strain Second Strain Trio Break Strain Trio

In "The Stars and Stripes Forever," the trio is played an
additional time. The piccolo plays a high accompanying part
(*obbligato*) the second time the trio is heard. The brasses play
additional harmony parts the last time. Each time it is
played, the trio becomes more exciting.

● Listen to "The Stars
and Stripes Forever."
How are the three
repetitions of the trio
like this painting
by Jasper Johns?

Three Flags by Jasper Johns

Three Flags. Jasper Johns, WHITNEY MUSEUM OF AMERICAN ART, New York.

 "The Stars and Stripes Forever" by John Philip Sousa

TAKE ANOTHER LOOK

American Music on Parade

During the Civil War, the U.S. was divided into two nations. One was the Union and the other was the Confederate States of America. Some of the songs of that era expressed strong loyalty to one of the two nations. Other songs were sung by people on both sides.

Soldiers sang while they marched to pass the time away, and to take their minds off the war and their families and friends back home. (Sing "Goober Peas" with the descant.)

Americans like to sing in times of peace, too. Whenever a band marches by, you may feel like singing and moving to the music. (Sing "Come, Follow the Band" with movement.)

Keeping the beat is part of the fun of singing. It is more exciting when you move as a group. (Sing "Madalina Catalina" with the movement game.)

A great song can express our hopes, our pride, and our love for our country. It often outlives the time for which it was written. (Sing "Battle Hymn of the Republic.")

168

JUST CHECKING

1. Which is the notation for four sounds equal to the length of one quarter note?

   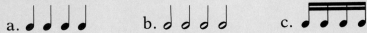

2. Below are all the markings for dynamic intensity that you have studied so far. Which marking indicates the softest sound? Which indicates the loudest sound?

   ff　　*p*　　*mf*　　*pp*　　*f*　　*mp*

3. Which group of dynamic marks shows the order from softest to loudest?

   a. *pp*　　*mp*　　*p*　　*mf*　　*ff*　　*f*
   b. *pp*　　*p*　　*mp*　　*mf*　　*f*　　*ff*

4. Which instruments are normally found in a band?

   a. tuba　　b. violin　　c. trombone　　d. saxophone

5. Which family of instruments is found in an orchestra but not in a concert band or marching band?

   a. woodwinds　　　　b. strings
   c. percussions　　　　d. brasses

UNIT 7 TWENTIETH CENTURY AMERICAN BEAT

During the twentieth century, many new styles of popular music have appeared across the United States. Ragtime and Dixieland Jazz began during the early 1900s. The Charleston became a popular dance during the 1920s. Swing and the "big band" sound developed during the 1930s and 1940s.

"Medley of American Musical Styles of the First Part of the Twentieth Century"

THE ROOTS OF JAZZ

Jazz styles of the twentieth century have many characteristics of spirituals and plantation songs. The syncopation and call-response patterns you often hear in jazz can be traced back directly to those early folk songs.

- Find the syncopation and the call and response in this black American spiritual.

Who Built the Ark?

Black American Spiritual

● Play this rhythm as you sing the melody of "Who Built the
Ark?" Choose instruments that can sound both long and
short.

AN OLD SONG IN A NEW STYLE

Dixieland bands played for political rallies, weddings, parties, and funerals. They played songs such as "When the Saints Go Marching In" as a slow march when they were going to the cemetery. Then they played it as joyous jazz on the way home. The happy music expressed the belief that the departed person had reached the promised land.

- Notice that when the melody is repeated, the note values are twice as long. This is called **augmentation.**

When the Saints Go Marching In

Traditional
Arranged by Mary Val Marsh

THE SOUND OF DIXIELAND BANDS

The early Dixieland band often marched as it played. The band usually had a cornet, a trombone, a clarinet, a banjo, drums, and sometimes a tuba. Later, the piano, saxophone, and trumpet were added.

New Orleans was the center of Dixieland music. Many musicians from all over the country traveled there to study this music.

Preservation Hall Jazz Band

"South Rampart Street Parade" was composed in the late 1930s, but it has the full flavor of an old-time New Orleans march. It was actually created in Chicago, where Bob Crosby's orchestra was playing. The New Orleans flavor was given by the drummer, who came from New Orleans.

 "South Rampart Street Parade" by Steve Allen, Ray Bauduc, and Robert Haggart

● Look and listen for a syncopated rhythm pattern.

Tiger Rag

Words and music by Jack Carey

Where's that Ti-ger? Where's that Ti-ger? Where's that Ti-ger?

Hold that Ti - ger   Hold that Ti - ger   Hold that Ti - ger

Hold that Ti-ger   Choke him, poke him, kick him and soak him!   Where's that Ti-ger?

Where's that Ti-ger?   Oh — where — can he   be?   Low or high brow,

they all cry   now,   Please play that Ti   -   ger Rag.

FERDINAND ("JELLYROLL") MORTON

Jellyroll Morton (1885–1941) was one of the first well-known jazz piano players. He played piano in a trio with drums and a clarinet. "Tiger Rag" was one of the pieces he made famous. Also a composer, Morton made many valuable contributions to the development of jazz.

James P. Johnson was a ragtime piano player. He played in Harlem for dance contests long before World War I. His early years in a dance band may have inspired him to write the music for the Charleston, a dance popular in the 1920s.

Charleston

Music by James P. Johnson
Words by Cecil Mack

Charles - ton __ Charles - ton __ Made in __ Car-o -

li - na __ Some dance, ____ some prance, ____

I'll say ____ there's no-thing fin - er than the Charles - ton, __

Charles - ton, __ lord how __ you can shuf - fle __

ev - 'ry step _ you do leads to some - thing new, man I'm tell - ing you

It's a la - pa-zoo, buck dance, _ wing dance, _

We'll be __ a back num - ber __ but the Charles - ton __ the new

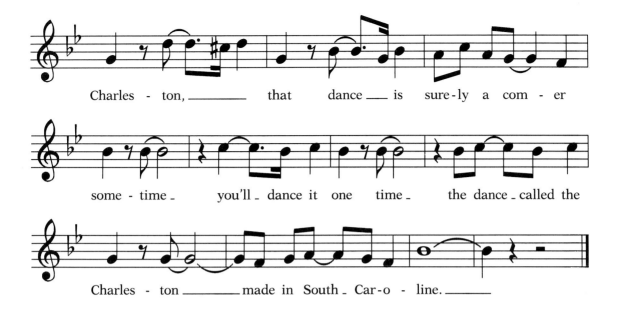

Charles - ton, _____ that dance ___ is sure-ly a com - er

some - time ___ you'll ___ dance it one time ___ the dance ___ called the

Charles - ton _____ made in South ___ Car-o - line. _____

- Learn to do the basic Charleston step. Move to the rhythm of the word "Charleston":

Measure 1

Step forward on your left foot and kick with your right foot

Measure 2

Step backward on your right foot and touch your left foot to the floor behind you

Cartoon by John Held, from the cover of *Life* magazine, 1926

- Continue this pattern throughout the song.
- Make up your own version of the Charleston step.

A NEW RHYTHM PATTERN

- Listen for the rhythm patterns that seem to shuffle along in this song.

Carolina in the Morning

Words by Gus Kahn
Music by Walter Donaldson

Noth - ing could be fin - er than to be in Car - o -
Stroll - ing with my girl - ie where the dew is pear - ly

li - na in the morn - ing,
ear - ly in the morn - ing,

No - one could be sweet - er than my sweet - ie when I
But - ter - flies all flut - ter up and kiss each lit - tle

meet her in the morn - ing.
but - ter - cup at dawn - ing.

1. Where the morn - ing glo - ries twine a - round my door, Whis - per - ing pret - ty sto - ries I long to hear once more.

2. If I had A - lad - din's lamp for on - ly a day, I'd make a wish and here's what I'd say: "No - thing could be fin - er than to be in Car - o - li - na in the morn - ing."

- Where in the song do you see measures made up entirely of the rhythm ♩. ♪ ?

MUSICAL INTERLUDE

An **interlude** is a short piece of music played between two longer sections of music.

● Play this body percussion as an interlude with the song "Macnamara's Band."

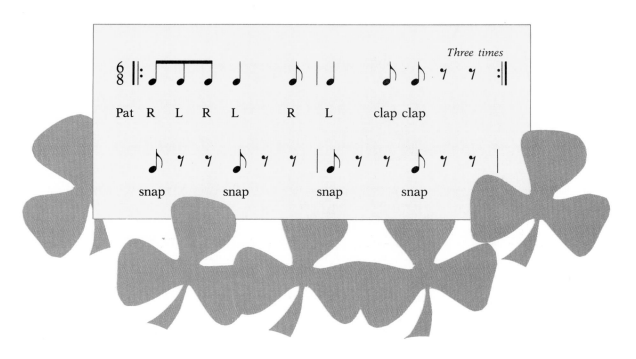

Macnamara's Band

Music by Shamus O'Connor
Words by John J. Stamford
American version by Red Latham,
Wamp Carlson, and Guy Bonham

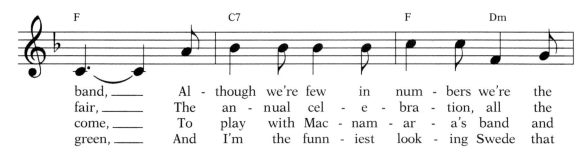

1. Oh! me name is Mac-nam-ar - a, I'm the lead-er of the
2. Right __ now we are re-hears-in' for a ver - y swell af -
3. Oh! my name is Un-cle Yul - ius and from Swe-den I have
4. Oh! I wear a bunch of sham-rocks and a un - i-form of

band, ____ Al - though we're few in num - bers we're the
fair, ____ The an - nual cel - e - bra - tion, all the
come, ____ To play with Mac - nam - ar - a's band and
green, ____ And I'm the funn - iest look - ing Swede that

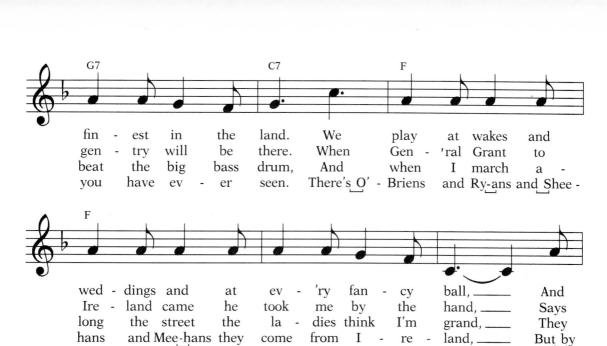

fin - est in the land. We play at wakes and
gen - try will be there. When Gen - 'ral Grant to
beat the big bass drum, And when I march a -
you have ev - er seen. There's O' - Briens and Ry-ans and Shee -

wed - dings and at ev - 'ry fan - cy ball, _____ And
Ire - land came he took me by the hand, _____ Says
long the street the la - dies think I'm grand, _____ They
hans and Mee-hans they come from I - re - land, _____ But by

when we play to fu - ner - als we play the march from Saul.
he, "I nev - er saw the likes of Mac - nam - ar - a's band."
shout, "There's Un - cle Yul - ius play - ing with an I - rish band."
Yim - min - y I'm the on - ly Swede in Mac - nam - ar - a's band.

Refrain

Oh! the drums go bang, and the cym - bals clang, and the horns they blaze a -

way; _ Mc - Car - thy pumps the old ba - zoon while I the pipes do play;

And, Hen - nes - sey Ten - nes - see too - tles the flute, and the mu - sic is some - thin'

grand; _ A cred - it to old I - re - land is Mac - nam - ar - a's band.

A SONG THAT'S JUST FOR FUN

● How do the rhythm and melody of this song give it a special "flavor" or style?

Mrs. Murphy's Chowder

Words and music by Oscar Brand

Won't you bring back, won't you bring back Mis-sus Mur-phy's chow-der? It was

tune-ful. Ev-'ry spoon-ful made you yo-del loud-er.

Af-ter din-ner, Un-cle Ben used to fill his foun-tain pen

From a plate of Mis-sus Mur-phy's chow-der.

Refrain
Faster

It had ice cream, cold cream, ben-zine, gas-o-line, Soup beans, string beans,
Sponge cake, beef-steak, mis-take, stom-ach ache, Cream puffs, ear-muffs,

float-ing all a-round; Silk hats, door-mats, bed slats, Dem-o-crats;
man-y to be found;

Cow-bells, door-bells beck-on you to dine; Meat-balls, fish balls,

moth-balls, can-non-balls. Come on in; the chow-der's fine!

JAZZ AND "SWING"

A dotted eighth note (♪.) sounds for the length of an eighth note plus half its length. A sixteenth note (♪) sounds for half an eighth note. They look like this ♪. ♫ when written together. These two combinations are equal in length:

● Look and listen for this combination in the next song:

On the Sunny Side of the Street

Words by Dorothy Fields
Music by Jimmy McHugh

Grab your coat   and get your hat,   Leave your wor-ries   on the

door - step,   Just   di - rect   your feet   To   the

sun - ny   side   of the street   Can't you   hear   a   pit - ter - pat?

And   that   hap - py   tune   is   your   step,

Life   can   be   so sweet   on   the sun - ny   side   of the street.

I used to walk in the shade ___ With those blues on pa-rade, ___ But I'm not a-fraid, ___ This rov-er crossed o-ver. If I nev-er have a cent, I'll be rich as Rock-e-fel-ler; Gold dust at my feet, On the sun-ny ___ side ___ of the street. ___

"Big bands" became popular during the 1930s, playing a kind of music called "swing."

Tommy Dorsey was known as the "Sentimental Gentleman of Swing." Many people thought his band played the best dance music. His band was famous for singing along with the band singer during parts of a song. Dorsey wrote this arrangement with Sy Oliver, a well-known music arranger and the leader of his own band.

● Listen for the big band sound.

 "On the Sunny Side of the Street," played by the Tommy Dorsey Band

Benny Goodman and Duke Ellington were two other popular leaders of big bands.

Benny Goodman played the clarinet and was known as the "King of Swing." He was one of the first jazz players to perform with a symphony orchestra.

Duke Ellington was creating his own jazz sounds as far back as 1924. His band mostly played music written by the Duke himself. In the 1940s his band recorded many of its greatest hits. One of these, "Take the A Train," became the Duke's theme song.

- Listen to two examples of the big band sound.

 "After You've Gone" by Benny Goodman and "Take the A Train" played by Duke Ellington and his band

Duke Ellington and his band

Self-portrait by George Gershwin

George Gershwin was the first American composer to combine jazz and classical music. Among his most famous works are "An American in Paris," "Rhapsody in Blue," and "Porgy and Bess."

● Listen to instrumental and vocal versions of "Summertime." How does the style differ in the two versions?

 "Summertime," from *Porgy and Bess* by George Gershwin (two versions)

From the 1935 premiere of *Porgy and Bess*

SINGING WITH RHYTHM

● Feel this rhythm pattern as you sing "It's Such a Joy."

It's Such a Joy

Studio singers of the thirties and forties performed live radio broadcasts as soloists and as members of ensembles.

The Old Wrangler and the Ranch Boys, popular radio entertainers of the 1930s

The Pointer Sisters, above, recording a song in a studio, and at left, performing for a television broadcast.

Today, solo and group singers usually record music for radio and television broadcasts. When they appear on TV, they very often mouth the words ("lip-sync") to the prerecorded sound.

PLAYING THE BELLS

- Play these notes on the bells.

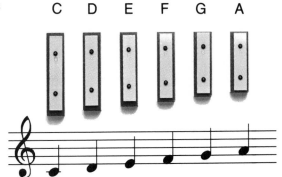

C D E F G A

- Play this song on the bells.

Pay Me My Money Down

Words and music by Lydia A. Parrish

C
1. I thought I heard the cap-tain say, "Pay me my mon-ey down,"

G7

G7
To-mor-row is our sail-ing day, — "Pay me my mon-ey down." —

C

Refrain

C
"Pay — me, — oh, pay — me, — Pay me my mon-ey down, —

G7

G7
Pay me or go to jail, — Pay me my mon-ey down." —

C

2. As soon as the boat was clear of the bar,
   "Pay me my money down,"
   He knocked me down with the end of
   a spar,
   "Pay me my money down."
   Refrain

3. Well, I wish I was Mr. Steven's son,
   "Pay me my money down,"
   Sit on the bank and watch the
   work done,
   "Pay me my money down."
   Refrain

FOLK PERCUSSION INSTRUMENTS

These are some common folk percussion instruments.

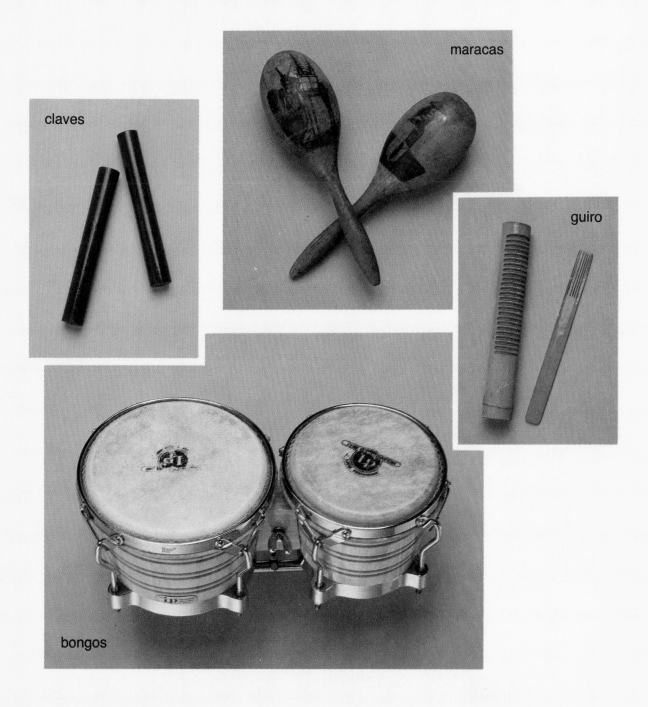

maracas

claves

guiro

bongos

● Use one of these instruments or a "found sound" created by objects in your classroom to accompany "Pay Me My Money Down."

TAKE ANOTHER LOOK

Twentieth Century American Beat

For most of the 20th century, American music has exerted a powerful influence on the popular music of the world. People everywhere sing American songs and dance to an American beat. Jazz was born in America. It grew slowly on American soil through a blending of African rhythms and European musical ideas. Jazz used the syncopated beat and the call-and-response improvisation of black work songs and spirituals. (Sing "Who Built the Ark?" and "When the Saints Go Marching In.")

When black people traveled North to find work, they took their music to new audiences. Large bands began to play a swinging dance beat. (Sing "On the Sunny Side of the Street.")

All music has the same basic elements. In European music, rhythm stayed in the background and melody and harmony remained more important. In America's jazz, the beat became as important as the other elements. (Sing "Pay Me My Money Down" and play the instrumental parts.)

JUST CHECKING

1. In $\frac{4}{4}$, how many beats does a quarter note get?

    a. 2   b. 4   c. 1

2. In $\frac{4}{4}$, which note sounds for 2 beats?

    a. ♩   b. ♩

    c. 𝅝   d. ♪

3. In $\frac{4}{4}$, which 2 notes equal 1 beat?

    a. ♫   b. ♩ ♩   c. ♩ ♩

4. Which notes are equal in length to ♫ ?

    a. ♫   b. ♪♩.   c. ♩. ♫

5. Which group of notes shows the order from longest to shortest sounds?

    a. ♩ ♩ ♪ 𝅝   b. ♪ ♩ ♩ 𝅝   c. 𝅝 ♩ ♩ ♪

6. Which note has the longest sound?

    a. ♩   b. ♩   c. ♪   d. 𝅝

7. Which note has the shortest sound?

    a. ♩   b. ♩   c. ♪   d. 𝅝

UNIT 8
THE AMERICAN BEAT GOES ON

A great variety of musical styles currently are being heard in the United States. They include folk music, jazz, rock-and-roll, music with a Latin American beat, disco, electronic music, experimental music, "classical" music, Broadway musicals, and music for movies and television.

SYMPHONY ORCHESTRAS

Over the past forty years there has been an increase in the number of symphony orchestras in the United States. Almost every major American city now has its own orchestra. Many cities have built beautiful auditoriums where these orchestras perform for the public.

During the summer, many orchestras perform at outdoor centers such as Tanglewood in western Massachusetts. Tanglewood is the summer "home" of the Boston Symphony.

Above, Carnegie Hall in New York City; left, Tanglewood, with outdoor and indoor seating available

A symphony orchestra has four families of instruments. They
are the string, brass, woodwind, and percussion families.

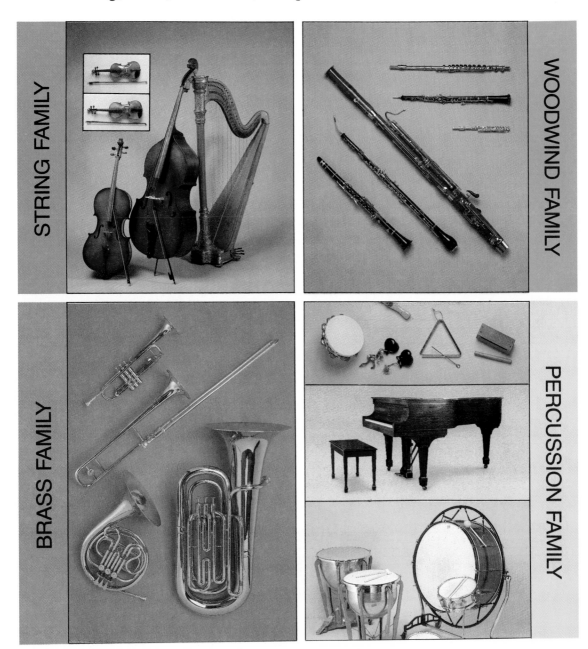

STRING FAMILY

WOODWIND FAMILY

BRASS FAMILY

PERCUSSION FAMILY

● Listen to Symphony No. 3 by Roy Harris. As you listen,
identify the families of instruments you hear.

 Symphony No. 3 by Roy Harris

This song is in a light pop style that was popular during the middle of the twentieth century.

- Listen to and look for the melody and the descant in "Isn't It Reassuring?"

Isn't It Reassuring?

Words and music by
Natalie Sleeth

Part I (second time only)

Spring - time! At last it's

Part II

Is - n't it re - as - sur - ing, ____

spring - time! The buds ap - pear, new ev - 'ry

watch-in' the buds ap - pear? Is - n't it great, ____

year, as if to cheer us, in ____ the

spring to a - wait, ____ watch-in' the land - scape ____ re - ju - ven - ate? O

spring - time, love - ly spring - time.

does-n't it lift your spir - it? ____ Does-n't it make you

O it's so keen to view the scene and watch the

glad? Is - n't it keen, _ view-in' the scene, _

grass ____ turn _ green. Gone the

watch-in' the grass_ turn green? The win-ter's gone now _ and the

snow that cov-ered seeds be-low and now the cold is

snow; seeds burst - in' be-low; cold's o - ver at

past and ev-'ry-thing can grow, __ for it's

last, and ev-'ry-thing's start-in' to grow!

spring - time! An - oth - er spring - time.

Does-n't it make you hap - py? __ Does-n't it make you

Part of the plan that came to man the mo-ment

see part of the plan __ giv-en to man, __

nice to see it hap - pen - ing, __ so good to see it

nice to see it hap - pen - ing, __ so good to see it

hap - pen - ing, __ just great to see it hap - pen - ing, __ a -

hap - pen - ing, __ just great to see it hap - pen - ing, __ a -

new, _____ a - new, _____

new, _____ a - new, _____

and re - as - sur - ing ___ too! _____

and re - as - sur - ing ___ too! _____

FOCUS ON

Natalie Sleeth

Natalie Sleeth was born in 1930 in Evanston, Illinois. She is a well-known composer of music that appeals to children and adults alike. Sleeth's musical training began at the age of four with piano lessons. Throughout high school, she performed in school concerts and with church choral groups. Sleeth attended Wellesley College, where she continued to study music. After graduating in 1952, she worked for several years as a church organist and music secretary.

It wasn't until 1970 that Sleeth began making her greatest contributions to the music world. After taking some composition classes at Southern Methodist University, she was encouraged to write her own music. Since then, over 120 of her compositions have been published, and she has received several musical awards. Her compositions are performed by many groups—from school choruses to the Mormon Tabernacle Choir. Sleeth is currently living in Denver, Colorado.

METER SIGNATURE

"Peanut Vendor" was written in the 1920s. It became popular again with a new big-band recording in the 1950s.

● Listen and join in singing as soon as you can.

Peanut Vendor

Music by Moises S. Rodriguez
Words by Marion Sunshine and L. Wolfe Gilbert

Big jum - bos, big dou - ble ones,
They're roast - ed, no ti - ny ones,

Come buy those pea - nuts roast - ed to - day.___
They're toast - ed, pea - nuts hot in the shell. __

Come try those fresh - ly roast - ed to - day! __
Come buy some. I eat more than I sell! __

If you're look - ing for a mor - al to ___ this song,
If an ap - ple keeps the doc - tor from __ your door,

D.C.

Fif - ty mil - lion lit - tle mon - keys can't __ be wrong.
Pea - nuts ought to keep him from you ev - er - more.

Coda

{ Pea - nuts! —
  *Ma - ni!*___ } We'll meet _ a - gain.   { Pea - nuts! —
                                              *Ma - ni!*___ } This street _ a - gain.

{ Pea - nuts! —
  *Ma - ni!*___ } You'll eat — a - gain.   { Pea - nuts! —
                                              *Ma - ni!*___ } That pea - nut man's gone.

In $\frac{4}{4}$ meter, the beats are grouped in sets of four. The **meter signature** at the beginning of a song shows how the beats are grouped.

The top 4 in this meter signature tells you that the beats are in groups of four.

The bottom 4 tells you that a quarter note sounds for one beat.

- What note sounds for two beats?
- What is the meter signature in "Peanut Vendor"?
- Tap on each beat as you sing "Peanut Vendor."

208

By the 1950s, the big bands were more popular than ever. Stan Kenton's band was well known for its high, wailing trumpets.

- Listen to the way the Stan Kenton Band plays "Peanut Vendor."

 "Peanut Vendor" by Moises S. Rodriguez played by the Stan Kenton Band

Stan Kenton was a well-known jazz bandleader in the late 1940s and the 1950s. The Stan Kenton Band, shown above, featured vocalist June Christy and sixteen musicians.

WEST SIDE STORY

West Side Story was a Broadway musical hit in the 1950s and a movie hit in the 1960s. Many different rhythms can be heard in the section of *West Side Story* called "Mambo." The mambo is a dance that originated in Latin America. It was very popular at the time *West Side Story* was written.

The composer Leonard Bernstein used the big band sound and the mambo rhythms to create a composition for symphony orchestra.

- Listen for the different sections of the orchestra in this music. Which are used the most? Why?

 "Dances" from *West Side Story* by Leonard Bernstein

LISTENING FOR METER

Strong and weak beats arranged in a repeated pattern create meter. Music in $\frac{4}{4}$ meter may be represented like this:

Some music is in $\frac{5}{4}$ meter. It has five beats in each group. This pattern is a combination of three beats and two beats and may be counted **1** 2 3 **1** 2. A quarter note sounds for one beat. A pattern in $\frac{5}{4}$ meter would look like this:

"Cool" jazz was developed in the 1950s by jazz groups such as the Dave Brubeck Quartet. "Take Five" was one of their hits. It is in $\frac{5}{4}$ meter.

● Listen to "Take Five." Pat on the strong beat (beat one) and the medium-strong beat (beat four).

 "Take Five" by Paul Desmond, played by the Dave Brubeck Quartet

SOUNDS OF THE SIXTIES

- Sing this song with a light tone color.

Fifty-Ninth Street Bridge Song
(Feelin' Groovy)

Words and music by
Paul Simon

Slow down, _ you move too fast. _ You got to make the morn -

- ing last. _ Just kick-in' down the cob-ble - stones, _

look-in' for fun and feel - in' groov - y. _____

Hel-lo lamp - post, what-cha know-in'? I've come to watch your flow -

-ers grow - in'. Ain't-cha got no rhymes ____ for me?

Doot-in' doo-doo, feel-in' groov - y. _____ Got

no deeds to do, no prom-is-es to keep. I'm dap-pled and drow-sy and

read-y to sleep. Let the morn-ing-time drop all its pet-als on me.

Life, I love you, All is groov - y. _____

Harry Partch was an original composer. He wanted sounds in his music that no instruments could play, so he invented his own instruments. He created one percussion instrument by cutting large glass jars in half and hanging them so that they could vibrate freely. These are called **cloud chamber bowls.** They sound a little like chimes.

- Listen for the cloud chamber bowls in "Cloud Chamber Music."

 "Cloud Chamber Music" by Harry Partch

Jamey Turner (b. 1940) has been a musician all his life. He began playing the clarinet and the piano at the age of six. Since then, he has also played wrench harps and musical saws. In the late 1970s he began playing glasses. His instrument is a set of over 50 special glasses partly filled with water. He touches their rims with dampened fingers to produce different tones.

- Listen to Jamey Turner playing *Adagio for Glass Harmonica.*

 Adagio for Glass Harmonica by Wolfgang Amadeus Mozart

A new instrument called a **synthesizer** was invented in the 1960s. It can reproduce the sound of almost any existing instrument. The inventor of the synthesizer was Robert A. Moog.

- Listen to "Pop Corn," a composition written for the synthesizer. What is its form? Which section is *legato?*

 "Pop Corn" by Gershon Kingsley

FLATS AND SHARPS

A **flat** (♭) lowers the pitch one half step.

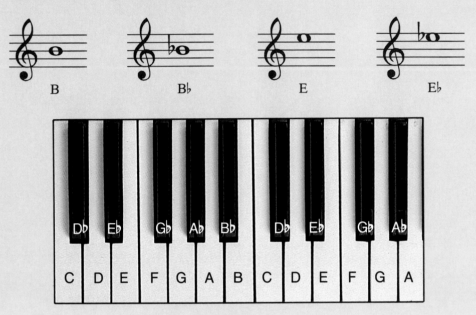

A **sharp** (♯) raises the pitch one half step.

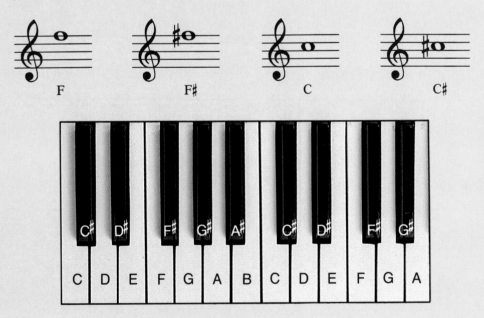

A **key signature** shows what pitches should be sharp or flat throughout the musical composition. When no sharps or flats appear in the key signature, the key is C.

To find the key of a musical composition, first look at the key signature. If the key signature has flats in it, locate the last flat to the right. Then count down three pitches. That pitch is the key.

- Look at this key signature and decide what key it is in.
- Read the scale and tell which pitches are flat.

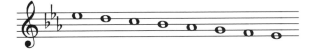

If the key signature has sharps in it, locate the last sharp to the right. Then count up one pitch. That pitch is the key of the composition.

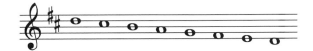

- In what key is this scale?
- Read the scale and tell which pitches are sharp.

In the 1960s and 1970s, folk and country music were as popular in the cities as in the country. Several singers combined both folk and country sounds. One of these singers, John Denver, sang "Thank God, I'm a Country Boy."

- Identify the flat in the key signature of "Thank God, I'm a Country Boy."
- In what key is this song?

Thank God, I'm a Country Boy

Words and Music by
John Martin Sommers

1. Well, life on a farm is kind-a laid back, ain't
2. When the work's all done and the sun's settin' low I

much an old coun-try boy like me can't hack. It's
pull out my fid-dle and I ros-in up my bow. But the

ear-ly to rise, ear-ly in the sack; Thank
kids are a-sleep so I keep it kind-a low; Thank

God, I'm a coun-try boy. A sim-ple kind-a life nev-er
God, I'm a coun-try boy. I'd play "Sal-ly Goodin'" all

did me no harm, Rais-in' me a fam-i-ly and
day if I could, but the Lord and my wife would-n't

work - in' on a farm. My days are all filled with an
take it ver - y good. So I fid - dle when I can and I

eas - y coun - try charm; Thank God, I'm a coun - try boy. ____
work when I should; Thank God, I'm a coun - try boy. ____

B

Refrain

Well, I got me a fine wife, I got me old fid - dle. When the

sun's com - in' up I got cakes ____ on the grid - dle; And

life ain't noth - in' but a fun - ny, fun - ny rid - dle; Thank

God, I'm a coun - try boy. ____

3. I wouldn't trade my life for diamonds or jewels,
   I never was one of them money hungry fools.
   I'd rather have my fiddle and my farmin' tools;
   Thank God, I'm a country boy.
   Yeah, city folk drivin' in a black limousine,
   A lotta sad people thinkin' that's mighty keen.
   Well, folks, let me tell you now exactly what I mean;
   Thank God, I'm a country boy. *Refrain*

4. Well, my fiddle was my daddy's till the day he died,
   And he took me by the hand and held me close to his side.
   He said, "Live a good life and play my fiddle with pride,
   And thank God you're a country boy."
   My daddy taught me young how to hunt and how to whittle,
   He taught me how to work and play a tune on the fiddle.
   He taught me how to love and how to give just a little;
   Thank God, I'm a country boy. *Refrain*

A BROADWAY MUSICAL OF THE 1970s

Rock was one of the most popular kinds of music during the 1970s. There was renewed interest in rock music styles of the 1950s. This interest was reflected in a Broadway hit musical called *Grease*.

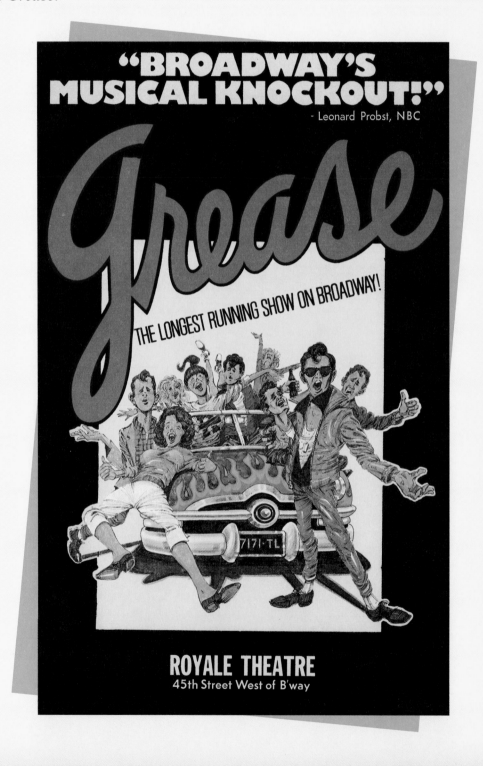

- Find the meter signature of "We Go Together." How many beats are in each measure? What note sounds for one beat?
- Look at the key signature. What key is this song sung in?

We Go Together

Words and music by
Jim Jacobs and Warren Casey

1. We go to-geth-er, like ra-ma la-ma la-ma ka
2. We're one of a kind ___ like dip ___ da dip ___ da dip

ding-a da ding-dong, Re-mem-bered for ev-er as
doo wop-a doo-bee doo, our ___ names are signed

shoo-bop sha-wad-da wad-da yip-pi-ty boom_de-boom
boog-e-dy boog-e-dy boog-e-dy boog-e-dy shoo-by doo wop_she bop

chang chang ah chang-it-ty chang-shoo bop, that's the way it should
chang chang ah chang-it-ty chang-shoo bop, we'll al-ways bee-ee like

be. ___ wha oooh, yeah!

one. Wa - wa - wa - waaah. When we go

out at night, and stars are shin - ing bright up in the

skies a - bove. Or at the high school dance

cresc. *f*

where you can find ro - mance, may - be it might be love.

Scenes from the movie version of *Grease*

We're for each oth - er like-a wop ba-ba lu-mop and wop bam boom.___

Just like my broth - er is sha - na - na na - na - na,

yip-pi-ty-dip - de doom   chang chang ah   chang-it-ty chang - shoo bop,

We'll al-ways be ___ to-geth - er, be to-geth - er.

VARIATIONS IN DYNAMIC LEVELS

The following composition was inspired by Olympic figure skating and by Igor Stravinsky's music for the ballet *Petrushka*.

- Listen for the different dynamic levels in this music. Pretend to skate with your pencil on a piece of paper. Skate in small circles for the softer part and larger circles for the louder sections. Your pencil should not leave the paper and should always be moving, creating a continuous line. How does your drawing compare with the painting shown here?

 "Petrushskates" by Joan Tower

Silverstone by Frank Stella

- Read this poem. Vary the dynamic level of your voice. Add instruments to emphasize the different levels of dynamics. Perform the poem.

SOME OPPOSITES

What is the opposite of riot?
It's lots of people keeping quiet.

The opposite of doughnut? Wait
A minute while I meditate.
This isn't easy. Ah, I've found it!
A cookie with a hole around it.

What is the opposite of two?
A lonely me, a lonely you.

The opposite of a cloud could be
A white reflection in the sea,
Or a huge blueness in the air,
Caused by a cloud's not being there.

The opposite of opposite?
That's much too difficult. I quit.
—*Richard Wilbur*

NEW MUSIC

This song was featured in the Opening Ceremonies of the Summer Olympics held in Los Angeles in 1984. The ceremonies were televised all over the world. The song became a symbol of the worldwide friendships that the Olympic Games encourage.

- Identify the meter and key of this song.
- Find the dotted eighth and sixteenth note pattern.

Reach Out and Touch (Somebody's Hand)

Words and music by
Nickolas Ashford and Valerie Simpson

Reach out and touch some - bod - y's hand, make this world a bet - ter place _____ if you can.

Reach out and touch some - bod - y's hand, make this world a bet - ter place _____ if you can.

(Just try)
1. Take a lit - tle time out of your bus - y day, To
2. If you see an old friend _____ on the street, and he's

give en-cour-age-ment to some-one who's lost the way.__
down, re-mem-ber, his shoes could fit your __ feet.__

(Just try) Or would I be talk-ing to a stone
Just try a lit-tle kind-ness and you'll __ see

if I asked you to share a prob-lem that's not your own __
it's some-thing that comes __ ver-y nat-ur-al-ly. __

__ We __ can change __ things if we start giv-ing.

Why don't you Why don't you (Why don't you)

reach out and touch some-bod-y's hand. ___

During the 1980s, composers have been trying different ways to write music. Some have tried to simplify music. Some composers have written music that is like the style of art called minimalism. Minimalist paintings and sculptures are simple and often have many repeated patterns. Philip Glass created music using these same ideas.

His music has become popular. He has become one of the best-known composers of this style of new music.

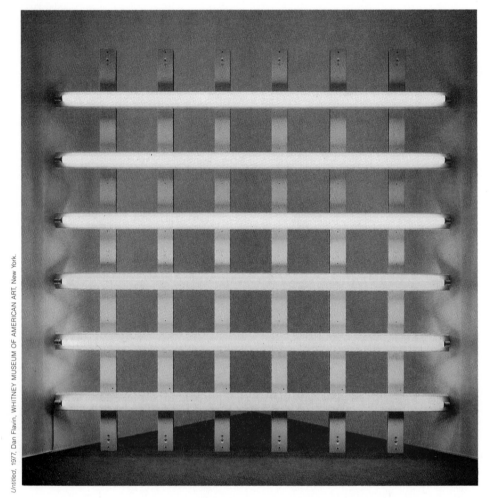

Untitled (For Robert with fond regards) by Dan Flavin. Horizontal fluorescent lights are mounted over vertical strips in this sculpture.

- Listen to a song by Philip Glass. Follow the words as you listen.

 "Lightning," with music by Philip Glass, and words by Suzanne Vega

Lightning

Philip Glass and Suzanne Vega

Lightning struck a while ago
And it's blazing much too fast
But give it rain or waiting time
And it will surely pass
Blow over

And it's happening so quickly
As I feel the flaming time
And I grope about the embers
To relieve my stormy mind
Blow over

Shaken this has left me
And laughing and undone
With a blinding bolt of sleeplessness
That's just begun
And a windy crazy running
Through the nights and through the days
And a crackling
Of the time burned away
Burned away

Now I feel it in my blood
All hot and sharp and white
With a whipcrack and a thunder
And a flash of flooding light

But there'll be a thick and smoky
Silence in the air
When the fire finally dies
And I'm wondering who'll be left there

In the ashes of the time
Burned away
Burned away

A GRAND FINALE

This year, you sang and listened to many different kinds of
American music. This patriotic song is appropriate to end the
year.

● Identify the meter signature and key for this song. Find the
dotted eighth and sixteenth note combination. Notice how
it adds to the exciting effect of the song.

This Is My Country

Music by Al Jacobs
Words by Don Raye

This is my coun-try! Land of my { birth. / choice. }

This is my coun-try! { Grand - est on earth. / Hear my proud voice. }

I pledge thee my al - le - giance, A - mer - i - ca the bold, for

This is my coun-try, to have and to hold!

- Learn these signs from American Sign Language.
- Sign the words as you sing "This Is My Country."

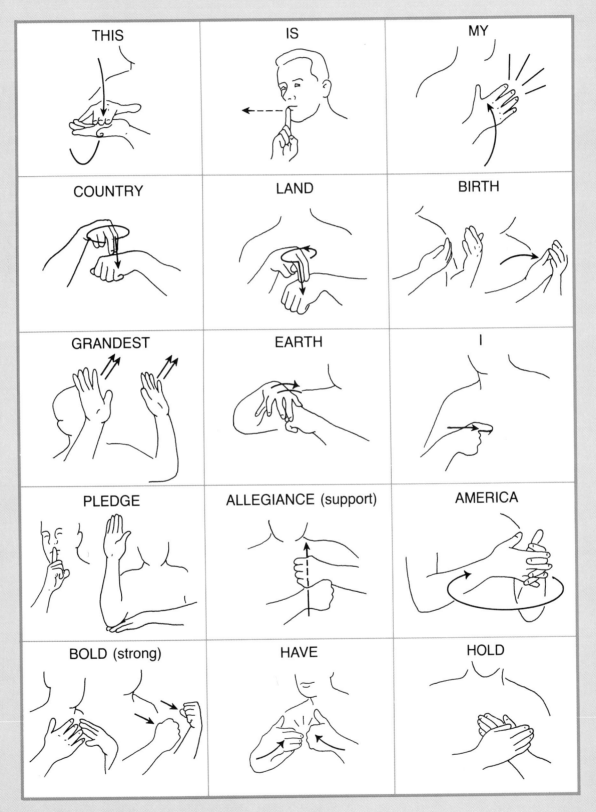

TAKE ANOTHER LOOK

The American Beat Goes On

America . . . a wonderful blend of many cultures.

   (Sing "Peanut Vendor.")

America . . . where we are free to hear and create any music we choose.

   (Sing "Isn't It Reassuring?")

America . . . where entertainment is an art.

   (Sing "We Go Together.")

America . . . where people can unite with people from other countries and sing of peace and friendship and helping one another.

   (Sing "Reach Out and Touch.")

No wonder that . . . the American beat goes on!

JUST CHECKING

1. What is the key signature?

2. What is the key signature?

3. What is the key signature?

4. Which of these meter signatures shows that the quarter note gets one beat?

   a. $\frac{2}{4}$ b. $\frac{2}{2}$

5. In which of these meter signatures would a half note sound for two beats?

   a. $\frac{2}{2}$ b. $\frac{2}{4}$

6. Which key signature shows that every F and every C is sharp?

   a.   b. 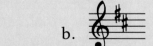   c.

7. Which key signature shows that every E is flat?

   a.   b.   c.

Charles Strouse

Charles Strouse has composed music for operas, ballets, symphony orchestras, and movies. However, he is best known for his work on Broadway shows, including *Bye Bye Birdie*, *Applause*, and *Annie*. His other works include the opera *Nightingale* and the ballet *Tunes*. He has won three Tony awards, two Grammy awards, and London's Best Musical award twice.

Mr. Strouse started to play the clarinet and the piano at the age of five and to compose music at the age of 15. He graduated from the Eastman School of Music in Rochester, New York, and later taught musical theater there.

Tomorrow

From the Broadway Musical *Annie*
Music by Charles Strouse
Words by Martin Charnin

The sun'll come out tomorrow,
bet your bottom dollar that tomorrow there'll be sun!
Jus' thinking about tomorrow
clears away the cobwebs and the sorrow till there's none.
When I'm stuck with a day that's gray and lonely,
I just stick out my chin and grin and say:
Oh! The sun'll come out tomorrow,
So you got to hang on till tomorrow come what may!
Tomorrow, tomorrow, I love ya tomorrow,
you're always a day away!

The sun'll come out tomorrow,
bet your bottom dollar that tomorrow there'll be sun!
Jus' thinking about tomorrow
clears away the cobwebs and the sorrow till there's none.
When I'm stuck with a day that's gray and lonely,
I just stick out my chin and grin and say:
Oh! The sun'll come out tomorrow,
Oh! I got to hang on till tomorrow come what may!
Tomorrow, tomorrow, I love ya tomorrow,
you're only a day away!

Tomorrow, tomorrow, I love ya tomorrow,
you're always a day away!
Tomorrow, tomorrow, I love ya tomorrow,
you're always a day away!

Tomorrow, tomorrow, I love ya tomorrow,
you're only a day away!
Tomorrow, tomorrow, I love ya tomorrow,
you're only a day away!

PIONEERING

A Musical Play by Hank Beebe

Pioneering

Words and music by Hank Beebe

Pi - o - neer - ing: _____

Pi - o - neer - ing:

Cov - ered wag - ons roll - ing 'cross a rock - y plain,
Still is done by peo - ple giv - ing it their best. Pi - o - neer - ing: _

Cov - ered wag - ons roll - ing 'cross a rock - y plain,
Still is done by peo - ple giv - ing it their best.

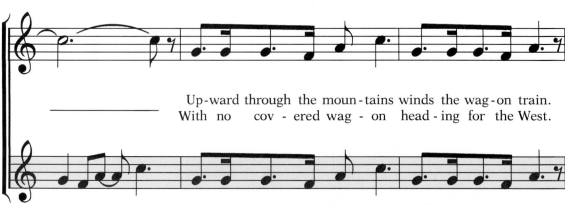

_____ Up - ward through the moun - tains winds the wag - on train.
With no cov - ered wag - on head - ing for the West.

Pi - o - neer - ing: Up - ward through the moun - tains winds the wag - on train.
With no cov - ered wag - on head - ing for the West.

Where no map will point the way, where no bridg-es stand,
Think-ing thoughts not thought be-fore, they plan what's not planned,

press-ing on-ward ev-'ry day, and reach-ing out
o-pen-ing a once-locked door and reach-ing out

for the prom-ised land.

Pi - o-neer - ing

land, prom - ised land,

Pi - o-neer - ing.

prom - ised land.

There are many kinds of pioneers besides the American
pioneers who traveled west. Astronauts are modern pioneers.

Unsung Heroes

First time: Part I unison   Words and music by Hank Beebe

Let us sing to un - sung her - oes,

Second time: Parts I and II

men and wo - men, chil - dren, too. Her - oes all, who

Let us sing to un - sung her - oes, men and wo - men,

stood for some - thing, some - thing good they had to do.

chil - dren too. Her - oes all who stood. _____

divisi

What they did is not for - got - ten; in our hearts they

2nd time to Coda
still be - long. So, to all the un - sung her - oes
f
loud - ly let us raise our song. Let us cel - e -
brate their cour - age, let us pay them our re - spect.
Give to them our ad - mir - a - tion; so our lives
their lives re - flect.
Coda
mf
Loud - ly let us raise loud - ly let us raise
mf
Loud - ly let us loud - ly raise
f
our song!

Anyone, from anywhere, can be a pioneer.

The Spice of America

First time: Part I unison
Second time: Part II unison
Third time: Parts I and II

Words and music by Hank Beebe

Va - ri - e - ty   is the

You'll meet a   young A - mer - i - can,

spice   of A - mer - i - ca, _____ the

old A - mer - i - can,   male A - mer - i - can,   fe-male A - mer - i - can,

pep-per and salt   that's nice   a-bout A - mer - i - ca. _____

tall A-mer - i-can,   short A - mer - i - can,   white A - mer - i - can,

_____ No   two peo-ple   look the same:___   a

black A-mer-i-can, Fran-co - A - mer-i-can, Ger-man-A-mer-i-can,

dif-f'rent face, a dif-f'rent name. It's al-ways new,

Si-no-A-mer-i-can, Ang-lo-A-mer-i-can, I-tal-o-A-mer-i-can, His-

nev-er the same thing twice._____ For

pan-o-A-mer-i-can, man-y more, to be pre-cise.__ For

in A - mer - i - ca va - ri - e - ty_____

in A - mer - i - ca va - ri - e - ty_____

1.,2. (to Part II) | 3.

_ is the spice. _ is the spice. __

(to Parts I and II)

_ is the spice. _ is the spice. __

A person does not have to travel to be a pioneer.

An inventor or a composer can be a pioneer.

A pioneer is someone who tries something new.

Up and Beyond

First time: Part I unison

Words and music by Hank Beebe

Up and be-yond   where I've ev-er been be-fore,
Up and be-yond   what I've ev-er been be-fore,

Second time: Part I and II

Up and be-yond

Up and be-yond _what I have known, _____ all of it now   is
Up and be-yond _ my wild-est dreams, _____ now I can be   so

Up and be-yond _____ my wild-est dreams,   Now I can be _

2nd time to Coda

out-side my door: the earth is a mar-ble, the o-cean a pond, so
ver-y much more: the wide world is call-ing, and I will re-spond, so

2nd time to Coda

_   so   much

watch me fly _____ up and be - yond. _____

Far and a-way are be-com-ing close and near, strange and bi-zarre, com-mon-place._

What was con-cealed is re-vealed loud and clear. For a time to be liv-ing

I'd pick to-day: That's my choice far and a - way. _____

⊕ Coda

Watch me fly _____ up and be - yond. _____

⊕ Coda

more. Watch me fly up and be - yond. _____

243

People can be pioneers in many different ways.

Reprise: Pioneering

(Sing verse two of "Pioneering" and use the second ending.)

SONGBOOK

The Boatman

Black American Folk Song

1. O the boat - man dance, the boat - man sing,
The boat - man up to ev - 'ry - thing.
When the boat - man come on shore,
He spend his mon - ey and he work for more.

2. Did you ever see where the boatman live?
His house in the hollow with a roof like a sieve!
Boatman say he got one wish.
If it gets much wetter he's going to be a fish.

3. The oyster boat should keep to shore.
The fishing smack should venture more
The sailing ship go before the wind,
The steamboat leave a trail behind.

John Kanaka

Traditional

I heard, I heard the old man say,

John Ka - na - ka, na - ka too - la - ay.

To - day, to - day is a hol - i - day,

John Ka - na - ka, na - ka too - la - ay.

Too - la - ay, too - la - ay,

John Ka - na - ka, na - ka too - la - ay.

Trampin'

Black American Spiritual

I'm tramp - in', tramp - in', Try-in' to make heav -en my home.

I'm tramp - in', tramp - in', Try-in' to make heav -en my home.

I've nev -er been to heav -en but I've _ been told, Try-in' to make heav -en my home.

That the streets up there are paved _ with gold, Try-in' to make heav -en my home.

I'm tramp - in', tramp - in', Try-in' to make heav -en my home.

I'm tramp - in', tramp - in', Try-in' to make heav -en my home.

Page's Train

North Carolina Folk Song

Pa-ge's train runs so fast, Can't see noth-ing but the win-dow glass.

Cumberland Gap

American Folk Song

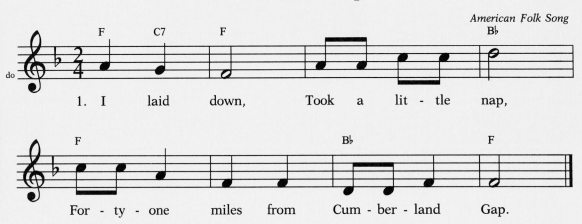

1. I laid down, Took a lit-tle nap,

For-ty-one miles from Cum-ber-land Gap.

2. Cumberland Gap's a mighty fine place,
   Can't get water to wash your face.

3. Cumberland Gap with its cliffs and rocks,
   Home of the panther, bear and fox.

Nine Hundred Miles

American Folk Song

1. Well, I'm walk-in' down this track, I've got tears in my eyes,

Try-in' to read a let-ter from my home._____

Refrain

And if this train runs me right I'll be home to-mor-row night,

'Cause I'm nine hun-dred miles from my home._____

2. Well, this train that I rode on, it's one hundred coaches long.
   You can hear the whistle sound for miles.
   Refrain

3. If my love she bids me stay, I will never go away.
   Near her I will always want to be.
   Refrain

Al Citron

Latin American Stone-passing Game

Al ci - tron de un fan - dan - go, san - go, san - go, sa - ba - ré.

Sa - ba - ré de la ron - de - la con su tri - ki, tri - ki trón.

● Name this tune.

Mystery Tune

Cape Cod Chantey

New England Sea Chantey

1. Cape Cod girls they have no combs, Heave a-way, Heave a-way;

They comb their hair with cod-fish bones, We are bound for Aus-tra-lia!

Refrain

Heave a-way my bul-ly, bul-ly boys, Heave a-way! Heave a-way!

Heave a-way and don't you make a noise, We are bound for Aus-tra-lia!

2. Cape Cod boys they have no sleds,
   Heave away, Heave away;
   They slide downhill on cod-fish heads,
   We are bound for Australia!
   Refrain

3. Cape Cod men they have no sails,
   Heave away, Heave away;
   They sail their boats with cod-fish tails,
   We are bound for Australia!
   Refrain

4. Cape Cod wives they have no pins,
   Heave away, Heave away;
   They pin their gowns with cod-fish fins,
   We are bound for Australia!
   Refrain

Sourwood Mountain

Appalachian Folk Song

1. Chick-en crow-in' on Sour-wood Moun-tain, Hey de-ing dang did-dle al-ly day.
2. My true love's — a blue-eyed dai-sy,

So man-y pret-ty girls I can't count them. Hey de-ing dang did-dle al-ly day.
If I don't — get — her I'll go cra-zy,

My true love she lives in Letch-er, Hey de-ing dang did-dle al-ly day.
My true love lives in the hol-low,

She won't come and I won't fetch her, Hey de-ing dang did-dle al-ly day.
She won't come and I won't fol-low,

Four in a Boat

American Singing Game

1. Four in a boat and the tide runs high,
2. Choose your ___ part - ner and stay all day,
3. Eight in a boat and it won't go 'round,

Four in a boat and the tide runs high,
Choose your ___ part - ner and stay all day,
Eight in a boat and it won't go 'round,

Four in a boat and the tide runs high,
Choose your ___ part - ner and stay all day,
Eight in a boat and it

Wait - ing for my pret - ty one to come by and by.
We ___ don't ___ care ___ what the old folk ___ say.

won't go 'round, And it sank to the bot - tom of the sea.

The Old Chisholm Trail

Cowboy Song
Words adapted by M.S.

1. Come a-long boys, and lis-ten to my tale.

I'll tell you of my trou-bles on the old Chis-holm trail.

Refrain

Come a ti yi yip-py, yip-py ay, yip-py ay, Come a ti yi yip-py, yip-py ay.

2. I woke one mornin' on the old Chisholm trail,
   A rope in my hand and a cow by the tail.
   Refrain

3. I started up the trail on October twenty-third,
   Started up the trail with the old cow herd.
   Refrain

4. On a ten dollar horse and a forty dollar saddle,
   I'm gonna punch those Texas cattle.
   Refrain

5. It's bacon and beans 'most ev'ry day,
   Just as soon eat prairie hay.
   Refrain

6. It's cloudy in the west and it looks like rain,
   Left my slicker in the wagon again.
   Refrain

7. My feet in the stirrups an' my seat in the saddle,
   I hung and rattled with the Texas cattle.
   Refrain

8. We rounded 'em up an' put 'em in the cars,
   An' that was the last of the old two bars.
   Refrain

9. I'm gonna see the boss, gonna get my money,
   Goin' back home to see my honey.
   Refrain

America, the Beautiful

Music by Samuel Ward
Words by Katharine Lee Bates
Arranged by Mary Val Marsh

1. O beau-ti-ful for spa-cious skies, For am-ber waves of grain.
2. O beau-ti-ful for pil-grim feet, Whose stern, im-pass-ion'd stress
3. O beau-ti-ful for he-roes proved In lib-er-at-ing strife,
4. O beau-ti-ful for pa-triot dream That sees be-yond the years,

For pur-ple moun-tain maj-es-ties, A-bove the fruit-ed plain,
A thor-ough-fare for free-dom beat A-cross the wil-der-ness.
Who more than self their coun-try loved, And mer-cy more than life.
Thine al-a-bas-ter cit-ies gleam Un-dim'd by hu-man tears.

A-mer-i-ca! A-mer-i-ca! God shed His grace on thee,
A-mer-i-ca! A-mer-i-ca! God mend thine ev-'ry flaw,
A-mer-i-ca! A-mer-i-ca! May God, thy gold re-fine,
A-mer-i-ca! A-mer-i-ca! God shed His grace on thee,

A-mer-i-ca!   A-mer-i-ca!

And crown thy good with broth-er-hood, From sea to shin-ing sea.
Con-firm thy soul in self con-trol, Thy lib-er-ty in law.
Till all suc-cess be no-ble-ness, And ev-'ry gain di-vine.
And crown thy good with broth-er-hood, From sea to shin-ing sea.

And crown thy good   From sea to shin-ing sea.
Con-firm thy soul,   Thy lib-er-ty in law.
Till no-ble-ness,   And ev-'ry gain di-vine.
And crown thy good   From sea to shin-ing sea.

255

You're a Grand Old Flag

Words and music by George M. Cohan
Arranged by Mary Val Marsh

Second time only: Part I

mf

There is a flag, a ver-y high fly-ing flag,

First time: All voices unison
Second time: Part II

f

You're a grand old flag, You're a high fly-ing flag, And for-

Ev - er will it wave,

ev - er in peace may you wave. You're the

It's the no-ble em-blem of the na-tion that we love,

em - blem of the land I love, the

(A few voices) Let her wave!

Free and brave,

home of the free and the brave, Ev-'ry

All hearts beat true be-fore the Red, White, and Blue,

heart beats true, un-der Red, White, and Blue, Where there's

Nev - er boast or brag, But should auld ac-quaint-ance

nev - er a boast or brag, But should auld *ac-quaint-ance

be for-got, just keep your eye on that

be for-got, keep your eye on that grand old flag.

flag, Keep your eye on that grand old flag!

flag, Keep your eye on that grand old flag!

*Optional third part

Fifty Nifty United States

Words and music by Ray Charles

Fif - ty nif - ty U - nit - ed States from thir - teen o - rig - i - nal col - o - nies;

Fif - ty nif - ty stars in the flag that bil - lows so beau - ti - f'ly in __ the breeze.

Each in - di - vid - u - al state con - trib - utes a qual - i - ty that is great.

Each in - di - vid - u - al state de - serves a bow, we sa - lute them now.

Fif - ty nif - ty U - nit - ed States from thir - teen o - rig - i - nal col - o - nies,

Shout 'em, scout 'em, Tell all a - bout 'em, One by one till we've

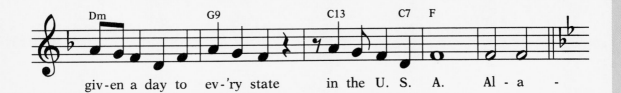

giv-en a day to ev-'ry state in the U. S. A. Al - a -

1st time: ♩=104 *2nd time: fast as possible*

bam - a, A - las-ka, Ar - i - zo - na, Ar - kan - sas, Cal - i -

for - nia, Col - o - ra - do, Con - nect - i - cut; Del - a - ware,

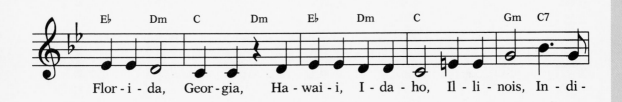

Flor - i - da, Geor - gia, Ha - wai - i, I - da - ho, Il - li - nois, In - di -

an - a; I - o - wa, Kan - sas, Ken - tuck - y, Lou - i - si -

an - a, Maine, Mar - y - land, Mas - sa - chu-setts, Mich - i - gan;

Min - ne - so - ta, Mis - sis - sip - pi, Mis - sou - ri, Mon -

tan - a, Ne - bras - ka, Ne - vad - a; New Hamp - shire,

New Jer - sey, New Mex - i - co, New York, North Car - o - li - na,

North Da - ko - ta, O - hi - o; Ok - la - ho - ma, Or - e - gon,

Penn - syl - va - nia, Rhode Is - land, South Car - o - li - na, South Da - ko - ta,

1st time: keep tempo at ♩=104 2nd time: ritard to ♩=152

Ten - nes - see, Tex - as; ___ U - tah, Ver - mont, Vir - gin - ia, Wash - ing - ton,

West Vir-gin-ia, Wis-con-sin, Wy - o - ming. Al - a - o - ming.

at beginning tempo ♩=152

North, south, east, west, in our calm, ob - jec-tive o - pin - ion, *(name of*

home state) is the best — of the Fif-ty nif-ty U - nit-ed States from

thir-teen o-rig-i-nal col - o -nies, Shout 'em, scout 'em, Tell all a-bout 'em,

One by one till we've giv-en a day to ev -'ry state in the good old

U. _____ S. _____ A. _____

Skin and Bones

Kentucky Folk Song
Collected by Jean Ritchie

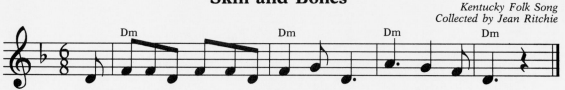

1. There was an old wom-an all skin and bones, OO - oo - oo - ooh!

2. She lived down by the old graveyard, Oo-oo-oo-ooh!

3. One night she thought she'd take a walk, Oo-oo-oo-ooh!

4. She walked down by the old graveyard, Oo-oo-oo-ooh!

5. She saw the bones a-layin' around, Oo-oo-oo-ooh!

6. She went to the closet to get a broom, Oo-oo-oo-ooh!

7. She opened the door and BOO!!

Pat-a-Pan

Early Burgundian French Carol

1. Wil - lie   take your lit - tle   drum, Rob - in bring your   flute   and

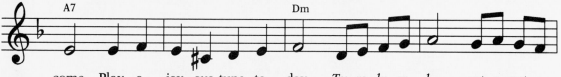

come. Play   a   joy-ous tune to - day.   *Tu - re - lu - re - lu,   pat - a - pat - a -*

pan, Play   a   joy-ous tune to - day on this joy-ous   hol - i - day.

2. When the little child was born long ago that Christmas morn
   Shepherds came from fields afar,
   Tu-re-lu-re-lu, pat-a-pat-a-pan,
   Shepherds came from fields afar guided by the shining star.

3. Now we celebrate this day on our instruments we play.
   Let our voices loudly ring,
   Tu-re-lu-re-lu, pat-a-pat-a-pan,
   Let our voices loudly ring, as our song and gifts we bring.

Fum, Fum, Fum

Catalonian Folk Song

1. On De-cem-ber twen-ty-fifth sing fum, fum, fum;

On De-cem-ber twen-ty-fifth sing fum, fum, fum.

On that day at ear-ly morn a lit-tle ba-by boy was born,

In a sta-ble dark and low-ly lay the in-fant Son most ho-ly, fum, fum, fum.

2. Christmas is a day of feasting, fum, fum, fum,
Christmas is a day of feasting, fum, fum, fum.
In hot lands and in cold, for young and old, for young and old,
We tell the Christmas story,
Ever singing of its glory, fum, fum, fum.

Winter Wonderland

Music by Felix Bernard
Words by Dick Smith

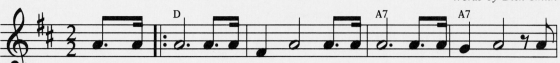

Sleigh bells ring are you list - 'nin'? In the lane snow is glist -'nin' A
way is the blue - bird, Here to stay is a new bird, He

beau - ti -ful sight,__ We're hap -py to -night __
sings a love song,__ As we go a -long __ Walk -in' in a win -ter won -der-

1. land! Gone a - 2. land! In the mead -ow we can build a

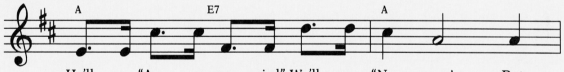

snow - man Then pre -tend that he is Par - son Brown.

He'll say "Are you mar - ried" We'll say "No man! But

you can do the job when you're in town." __ Lat - er on we'll con-

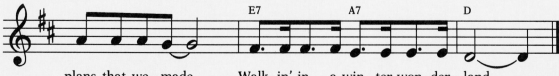

spire _ as we dream by the fire __ To face un -a -fraid _ the

plans that we made _ Walk -in' in a win -ter won -der - land. ___

264

Go, Tell It on the Mountain

Black American Spiritual

1. When I was a seek-er, I sought both night and day.
2. He made me a watch-man Up-on the cit-y wall.
3. In the time of Da-vid, Some said he was a king.

I asked the Lord to help me, And He showed me the way. __
And if I serve Him tru-ly, I am the least of all. __
And if a child is true born, The Lord will hear him sing. __

Refrain

Go, tell it on the moun-tain, O-ver __ the hills and ev-'ry-where.

Go, tell it on the moun-tain, Our heav'n-ly Lord __ is born.

The Twelve Days of Christmas

Traditional English Carol

1. On the first day of Christ-mas my true love sent to me: A

par-tridge__ in a pear tree. 2. On the sec-ond day of Christ-mas my

true love sent to me: Two tur-tle doves and a par-tridge__ in a pear tree.

3. On the third day of Christ-mas my true love sent to me:

Three French__hens, two tur-tle doves and a par-tridge__ in a pear tree.

4. On the fourth day of Christ-mas my true love sent to me:

{ Four col - ly birds,
three French __ hens, } two tur-tle doves and a par-tridge in a pear tree.

5. On the fifth day of Christ-mas my true love sent to me:

Five gold-en rings, four _ col-ly birds, three French hens,

two _ tur-tle doves, and a par-tridge in a pear tree.

6.–12. On the sixth day of Christ-mas my true love sent to me:
(etc.)

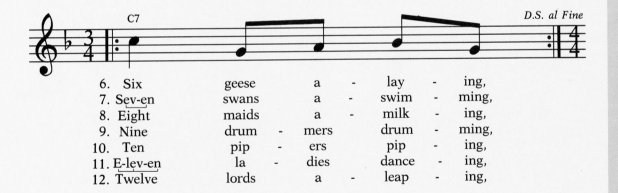

6. Six	geese	a -	lay - ing,
7. Sev-en	swans	a -	swim - ming,
8. Eight	maids	a -	milk - ing,
9. Nine	drum - mers	drum -	ming,
10. Ten	pip - ers	pip -	ing,
11. E-lev-en	la - dies	dance -	ing,
12. Twelve	lords	a -	leap - ing,

Casey Jones

Music by Eddie Newton
Words adapted by M. S.

1. Come, all you round-ers for I want you to hear

The sto - ry of a brave _ en - gi - neer.

Cas - ey Jones _____ was the round - er's name

On a big eight wheel - er of a might - y fame.

Refrain

Cas - ey Jones mount - ed to his cab - in,

Cas - ey Jones, with his or - ders in his hand,

Cas - ey Jones mount - ed to his cab - in

When he took his fa - mous trip _ to the prom - ised land.

2. The caller called Casey 'bout a quarter to four,
   He kissed his wife at the station door.
   He climbed to the cabin with his orders in his hand,
   When he took his famous trip to the promised land.
   Refrain

3. Eighty miles an hour down the Reno hill,
   The whistle was a cryin' out loud and shrill.
   The switchman knew by the engine's moans,
   That the man at the throttle was Casey Jones.
   Refrain

4. Casey saw that the signal was red,
   The eastbound freight was broken down ahead.
   He shouted to the fireman, "Man, you'd better jump,
   'Cause there's two locomotives that are gonna bump."
   Refrain

5. Casey knew that things could never be worse,
   He slammed on the brakes and made the wheels reverse.
   Casey Jones was soon to meet his fate,
   As he crashed his locomotive with the eastbound freight.
   Refrain

Cotton-Eyed Joe

American Dance Tune

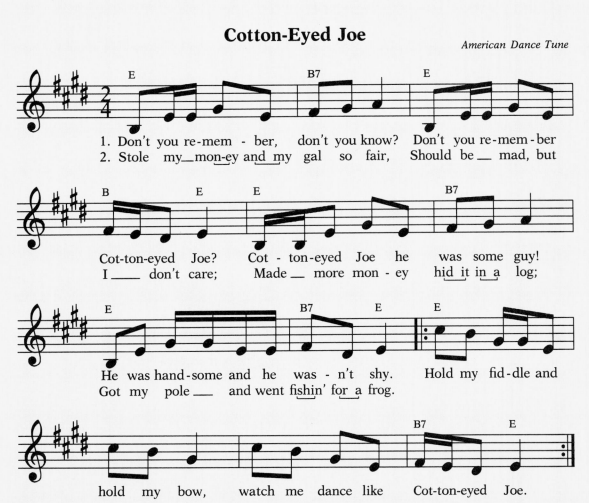

1. Don't you re-mem - ber, don't you know? Don't you re-mem-ber
2. Stole my mon-ey and my gal so fair, Should be mad, but

Cot-ton-eyed Joe? Cot - ton-eyed Joe he was some guy!
I don't care; Made more mon-ey hid it in a log;

He was hand-some and he was-n't shy. Hold my fid-dle and
Got my pole and went fishin' for a frog.

hold my bow, watch me dance like Cot-ton-eyed Joe.

269

Eight Bells

Sea Chantey

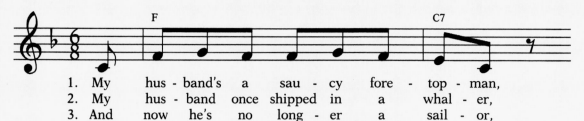

1. My hus-band's a sau-cy fore-top-man,
2. My hus-band once shipped in a whal-er,
3. And now he's no long-er a sail-or,

A chum of the cook's don't you know, _____
And sailed to the far north-ern seas, _____
He of-ten wakes up in the night, _____

He bel-lowed in-to the cook's fun-nel,
But be-ing a good heart-ed sail-or,
And think-ing he's still on the whal-er,

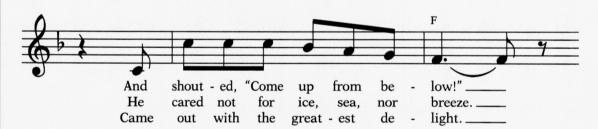

And shout-ed, "Come up from be-low!" _____
He cared not for ice, sea, nor breeze. _____
Came out with the great-est de-light. _____

Refrain

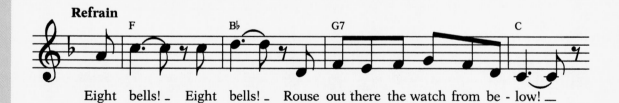

Eight bells! _ Eight bells! _ Rouse out there the watch from be-low! _

Eight bells! _ Eight bells! _ Rouse out there the watch from be-low! _

Hava Nashira

Israeli Round

Ha - va na - shi - ra, Shir al - le - lu - ia!

Ha - va na - shi - ra, Shir al - le - lu - ia!

Ha - va na - shi - ra, Shir al - le - lu - ia!

Hey, Ho! Anybody Home?

Traditional Round

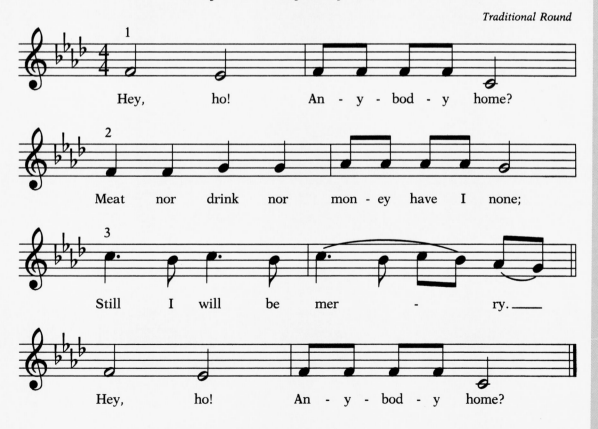

Hey, ho! An - y - bod - y home?

Meat nor drink nor mon - ey have I none;

Still I will be mer - ry. ___

Hey, ho! An - y - bod - y home?

It's the Hard-Knock Life

From the Broadway Musical Annie

It's the hard-knock life for us!
It's the hard-knock life for us!
'Stead a treated we get tricked,
'Stead a kisses we get kicked,
It's the hard-knock life!
Got no folks to speak of, so
It's the hard-knock row we hoe
Cotton blankets 'stead a wool,
Empty bellies 'stead a full,
It's a hard-knock life.
Don't it feel like the wind is always howlin'?
Don't it seem like there's never any light?
Once a day don't you want to throw the towel in?
It's easier than puttin' up a fight.
No one's there when your dreams at night get creepy,
No one cares if you grow, or if you shrink,
No one dries when your eyes get wet and weepy.
From the cryin' you would think this place would sink.
Oh! Santa Claus we never see,
Santa Claus, what's that? Who's he?
No one cares for you a smidge
When you're in an orphanage,
It's a hard-knock life (Yes it is)
It's the hard-knock life. (Yes it is)
It's the Hard-knock Life.

Music by Charles Strouse
Words by Martin Charnin

Funga Alafia

Liberian Welcome Dance

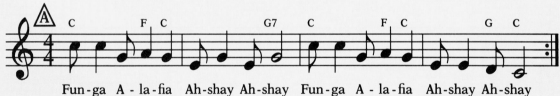

Fun-ga A-la-fia Ah-shay Ah-shay Fun-ga A-la-fia Ah-shay Ah-shay

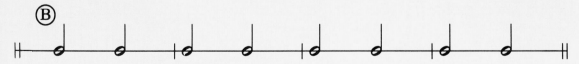

Mango Walk

Jamaican Calypso

My moth-er deed-a tell me that you go man-go walk, you

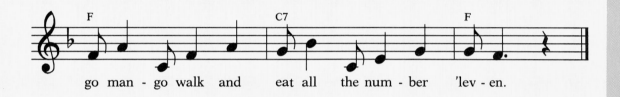

go man-go walk, you go man-go walk. My moth-er deed-a tell me that you

go man-go walk and eat all the num-ber 'lev-en.

Shalom Chaverim

Israeli Round

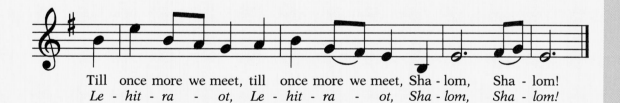

Sha-lom, good _friends, Sha-lom, good _friends, Sha-lom, Sha-lom!
Sha-lom, cha-ve-rim, Sha-lom cha-ve-rim, Sha-lom, Sha-lom!

Till once more we meet, till once more we meet, Sha-lom, Sha-lom!
Le-hit-ra-ot, Le-hit-ra-ot, Sha-lom, Sha-lom!

Snowbird

Words and music by Gene MacLellan

Be - neath this snow-y man-tle cold _ and clean _____ the
un - born grass lies wait-ing for its coat to turn to green. ___
_____ The Snow-bird sings the song he al - ways sings ____
___ and speaks to me of flow-ers that will bloom a - gain in
spring. ___ 2. When flow. ___ Yeah ___ If I could _ you know ___ that I would
fly _____ a - way with you.

2. When I was young my heart was young then too,
   And anything that it would tell me, that's the thing that I would do.
   But now I feel such emptiness within
   For the thing I want the most in life is the thing that I can't win.

3. Spread your tiny wings and fly away,
   And take the snow back with you where it come from on that day.
   The one I love forever is untrue,
   And if I could you know that I would fly away with you.

4. The breeze along the river seems to say,
   That he'll only break my heart again should I decide to stay.
   So, little Snowbird, take me with you when you go
   To that land of gentle breezes where the peaceful waters flow.

274

Texas, Our Texas

Music by William J. Marsh
Words by Gladys Yoakum Wright
Descant by Mary Val Marsh

Allegro maestoso (with steady march rhythm—not fast)
(Optional descant—Use verse 3 only if more than one verse is used)

1. Tex - as, our Tex - as, All hail, might - y state!
3. Tex - as, dear Tex - as, From ty - rant now free.

Melody

1. Tex - as, our Tex - as! All hail the might - y state!
2. Tex - as, O Tex - as! Your free-born sin - gle star,
3. Tex - as, dear Tex - as! From ty - rant grip now free,

Tex - as, our Tex - as, So won - drous great.
Shines forth in splen - dor Your des - ti - ny!

Tex - as, our Tex - as! So won - der - ful so great!
Sends out its ra - diance To na - tions near and far,
Shines forth in splen - dor Your star of des - ti - ny!

Bold and grand - est, A - gainst each test; O
Mo - ther of he - roes, Your child - ren true Pro -

Bold - est and grand - est, With - stand - ing ev - 'ry test; O
Em - blem of free - dom! It sets our hearts a - glow, With
Mo - ther of he - roes! We come your chil - dren true, Pro -

Descant © Copyright 1981 by Mary Val Marsh.

275

Em - pire wide and glo - rious, Su - preme - ly blest.
claim - ing our al - le - giance, Our love for you.

Em - pire wide and glo - rious, You stand su - preme - ly blest.
thoughts of San Ja - cin - to And glo - rious Al - a - mo.
claim - ing our al - le - giance Our faith our love for you.

21

God bless Tex - as! And keep you strong, That

God bless you Tex - as! And keep you brave and strong, That

you may grow Through - out ag - es long.

you may grow in pow'r and worth, Through - out the ag - es long.

29

God bless Tex - as! And keep you strong, That

God bless you Tex - as! And keep you brave and strong, That

you may grow _____ Through-out the ag - es long.

you may grow in pow'r and worth, Through-out the ag - es long.

Pat Works on the Railroad

American Railroad Song

1. In eight-een hun-dred and for-ty-one, I put me cord-'roy breech-es on,
2. In eight-een hun-dred and for-ty-two, I left the old world for the new,
3. In eight-een hun-dred and for-ty-three, 'twas then I met sweet Bid-dy Ma-gee,

I put me cord-'roy breech-es on, To work up-on the rail-way.
'Twas sor-ry luck that brought me through To work up-on the rail-way.
And an el-e-gant wife she's been to me while work-in' on the rail-way.

Refrain

Fil - li - me - oo - re - i - re - ay, Fil - li - me - oo - re - i - re - ay,

Fil - li - me - oo - re - i - re - ay, To work up - on the rail - way.

277

Talking Dust Bowl

Words and music by Woody Guthrie

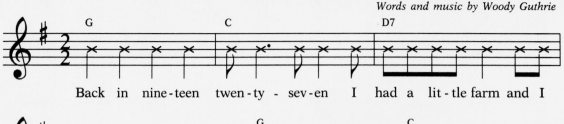

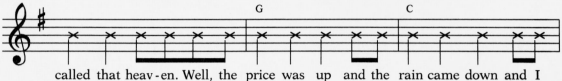

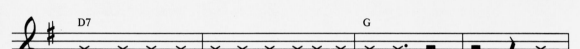

2. Rain quit and the wind got high,
   And a black old dust storm filled the sky,
   And I swapped my farm for a Ford machine,
   And I poured it full of this gasoline.
   And I started - rocking and a-rolling -
   Over the mountains out towards the old peach bowl.

3. Way up yonder on a mountain road,
   I had a hot motor and a heavy load,
   I was going pretty fast, I wasn't even stopping,
   A-bouncing up and down like a popcorn popping.
   Had a breakdown - a sort of a nervous bust-down of some kind.
   There was a fellow there, a mechanic fellow,
   said it was engine trouble.

4. We got out to the West Coast broke,
   So dad gum hungry I thought I'd croak,
   And I bummed up a spud or two,
   And my wife fixed up a 'tater stew.
   We poured the kids full of it. Mighty thin stew, though;
   You could read a magazine right through it.

5. Always have figured that if it had been
   just a little bit thinner some of
   these here politicians could have seen
   through it.

Vine and Fig Tree

Music by Shalom Altman
Hebrew Words from Isaiah 2:4
English version by Leah Jaffa and Fran Minkoff

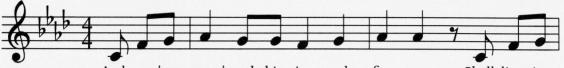

And ev-'ry man 'neath his vine and fig tree, Shall live in
Lo yi-sa goy el___ goy che-rev,___ Lo yil-m'-

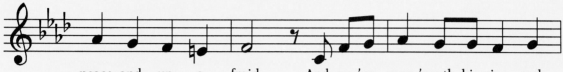

peace and un-a-fraid And ev-'ry man 'neath his vine and
du od mil-cha-ma Lo yi-sa goy el___ goy che-

Fine

fig tree Shall live in peace and un-a-fraid
rev___ Lo yil-m'-du od mil-cha-ma

And in-to plough-shares turn their swords Na-tions shall learn war no more
Lo yi-sa goy el goy che-rev, Lo yil-m'-du od mil-cha-ma

D. C. al Fine

And in-to plough-shares turn their swords Na-tions shall learn war no more.
Lo yi-sa goy el goy che-rev, Lo yil-m'-du od mil-cha-ma

Vive la Canadienne

French Canadian Folk Song

1. Vi - ve la Ca - na - dien — ne! Vo - le, mon coeur,

vo — le! Vi - ve la Ca - na - dien — ne Et

ses jo - lis yeux doux, Et ses jo - lis yeux

doux, doux, doux, Et ses jo - lis yeux doux. ___

2. On danse avec nos blondes,
   Vole, mon coeur, vole!
   On danse avec nos blondes;
   Nous changeons tour à tour,
   Nous changeons tour à tour, tour, tour,
   Nous changeons tour à tour.

We Watch TV

1. How do we play when we get our own way?
   We just watch TV.
   We sit in a heap as we try not to sleep,
   When we watch TV.
   As we spin the dial and give each show a trial,
   From cartoons to MTV;
   We never admit that we get tired of it,
   As we watch TV.

2. Homework is done now our favorite fun
   Is to watch TV.
   Violence and guns and too many reruns,
   As we watch TV.
   We're searching to find how to improve the mind,
   So we switch to cable TV.
   A silly new game and much more of the same,
   As we watch TV.

3. Weather reports and our favorite sports,
   As we watch TV.
   We get different views of the national news,
   As we watch TV.
   Republicans, Democrats all have their say,
   Thank goodness it's all there for free.
   It's sometimes a bore but we cannot ignore
   What is on TV, on TV,
   Watch TV, Watch TV.

Music by Charles B. Ward
Words by M.S.

281

Winter Song

Words and music by Stephen Paulus

Bells __ are ring - ing, they're ring - ing for ev - 'ry - one;

Play - ing a song that is bright as the morn - ing sun.

Bells __ are ring - ing, they're ring - ing for you and me,

Play - ing a light and a won - der - ful mel - o - dy.

Sing, sing a win - ter song, Sing, sing a hap - py song.

Ring, ring, ring, ring, ching ring. _____

1. Win - ter songs __ are for ev - 'ry one, _____
2. Long __ nights __ and cold win - try winds, _____

Young, Old, peo - ple so wear - y, Young, Old,
Snow, snow, i - ci - cles long, _____ warm to

peo - ple so cheer - y who Sing, sing, sing, sing.
win - ter's song ___ so Sing, sing, sing, sing.

Sing, sing a win - ter song, ___

Bells ___ are ring - ing, they're ring - ing for you and me,

Sing, sing a hap - py song, ___

Play - ing a light and a won - der - ful mel - o - dy.

Ring, ring, ring, ring, Ring, ring, ring, ring,

Ring, ring, ring, ring, Ring, ring, ring, ring,

Ring, ring, ring, ring, Ring! ___

Ring, ring, ring, ring, Ring! ___

MORE CHORAL MUSIC

Singing in chorus is an exciting musical experience. It provides the opportunity to blend your voice with others' to produce beautiful music.

In this section, you will learn techniques that will help you develop your voice and your singing ability. You will learn songs written in different languages representing different musical styles and periods. Learning to sing these songs expressively, together with the other choral skills you learn, will prepare you to participate in joyous singing experiences for the rest of your life.

Preparation for Singing: Crawdad Hole

In this arrangement of the American folk song "Crawdad Hole," the melody is accompanied by two other melodies called countermelodies.

● Establish the tonality of G major by singing up and down its scale and continuing down to D.

● Sing the following sequence of melodic patterns, which will help you to learn the lower countermelody of "Crawdad Hole."

- Clap the following rhythm pattern from "Crawdad Hole."

- Now find the rhythm pattern in the lower countermelody of the song and sing those two measures.

Crawdad Hole

Freely, quasi recitative

Part I — Well, you get a line, We'll go fish-in' in a craw-dad hole!

Part II — Well, you get a line and I'll get a pole, We'll go fish-in' in a craw-dad hole!

Allegretto (♩=110) *First time: Part I Unison* *Second time: Parts I and II*

You get a line and I'll get a pole, Hon-ey.

Get a pole and let's go fish-in', my hon-ey, my ba-by,

You get a line and I'll get a pole, Babe.

Get a pole and let's go fish-in', my hon-ey, my ba-by,

CRAWDAD HOLE American Folk Song
Arrangement for 3 pt. Treble Voices by Mary Goetz. © Copyright 1986 by Boosey & Hawkes, Inc. Reprinted by permission of Boosey & Hawkes, Inc.

You get a line and I'll get a pole, We'll go fish-in' in a craw-dad hole, _

Get a pole and let's go fish-in', my hon-ey, my ba-by,

9

1. **2.**

Hon-ey, Ba - by mine! Well mine! Well

Let's go now, come on, _ come on, get your pole, let's go!

12 *Part III optional* *mf*

Catch me a horse-fly, _____

what you gon-na do if the pond is dry, _ Hon-ey? _____

mp

Get a pole and let's go fish-in', my hon-ey, my ba-by,

Hook, line and sink-er, _____ Hook, line and sin-ker. __

Hon-ey, Ba - by mine,

Let's go now, come on, _come on, get a pole, let's go!

_ Let's go, get your pole, let's go!

Hon-ey, Ba - by mine, _____ let's go!

Let's go now, come on, _come on, get your pole, let's go!

Preparation for Singing: Midnight

The text of "Midnight" is based on an old nursery rhyme.

- Read the text and find the humorous statements.
- Sing the following melodic patterns on "loo" to
  help you establish the tonality of "Midnight."

Midnight

Words and music by Robert Starer

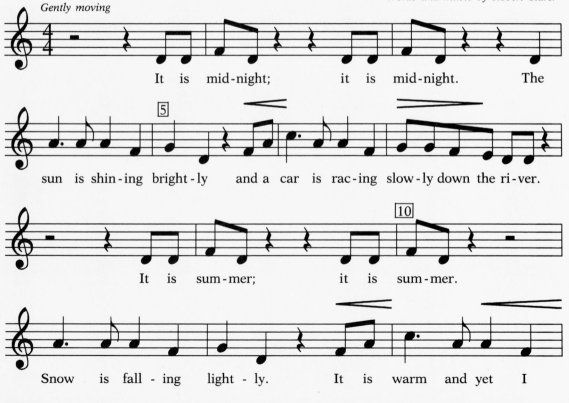

Preparation for Singing: Cuckoo!

Benjamin Britten, a famous twentieth-century English composer, wrote this song for the students of a boys' school in England.

● Warm up your voice by singing the following exercise. Keep your jaw relaxed. Sing it one time using "weh" and the second time using "way."

Weh — (breathe) Weh — (breathe) Weh — (breathe) Weh — (breathe)
Way —   Way —   Way —   Way —

Cuckoo!

Music by Benjamin Britten
Words by Jane Taylor

Cuc-koo,   Cuc-koo,   What do you do?_____

Cuc-koo,   Cuc-koo,   Cuc-koo,   Cuc-koo,

"In A - pril I o-pen my bill; In

Cuc-koo,   Cuc-koo,   Cuc-koo,   Cuc-koo,

Preparation for Singing: Alleluia

"Alleluia" is from a cantata that Johann Sebastian Bach wrote in 1712 for the first day of the Christmas celebration.

- Sing this echo pattern, focusing on the pure vowels in the word "alleluia" (ah, eh, and oo). Be sure your jaw is relaxed.

In some words, a syllable has two vowel sounds called diphthongs. The words "voi-ces" and "joy," found in "Alleluia," contain the "oy" sound. This diphthong is made up of the vowel sounds "aw" plus "ee." The words "day," "praise," and "name" contain the "ay" sound. This diphthong is made up of the vowel sounds "eh" plus "ee."

$$oy = aw + ee \qquad ay = eh + ee$$

- Sing the following phrase using the pure vowels "aw" and "eh." Only put in the "ee" at the last second.

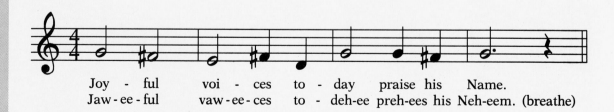

Alleluia

Music by J. S. Bach
Arranged by Channing Lefebvre
English version by Sydney Biden

ces;
de;

Thou God to -
denn Gott hat

day
heut'

hast giv'n us joy,
ge - macht solch' Freud',

Hold fast to Him And praise His
der wir ver - ges - sen soll'n zu

Name e - ter - nal.
kei - ner ___ Stun - de.

PLAYING THE RECORDER

● Play B. ● Play A. ● Play G.

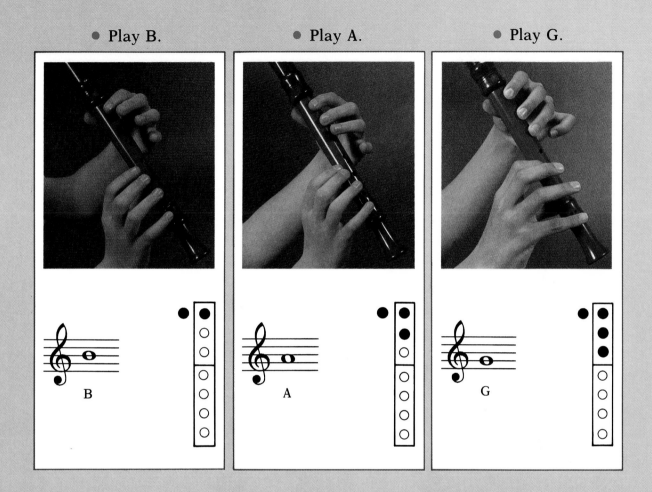

● Play each pitch as a long tone. Use a steady breath. Make the sound

SMOOTH

not

WAVY.

● Measure the length of your note. How long can you hold a good sound?

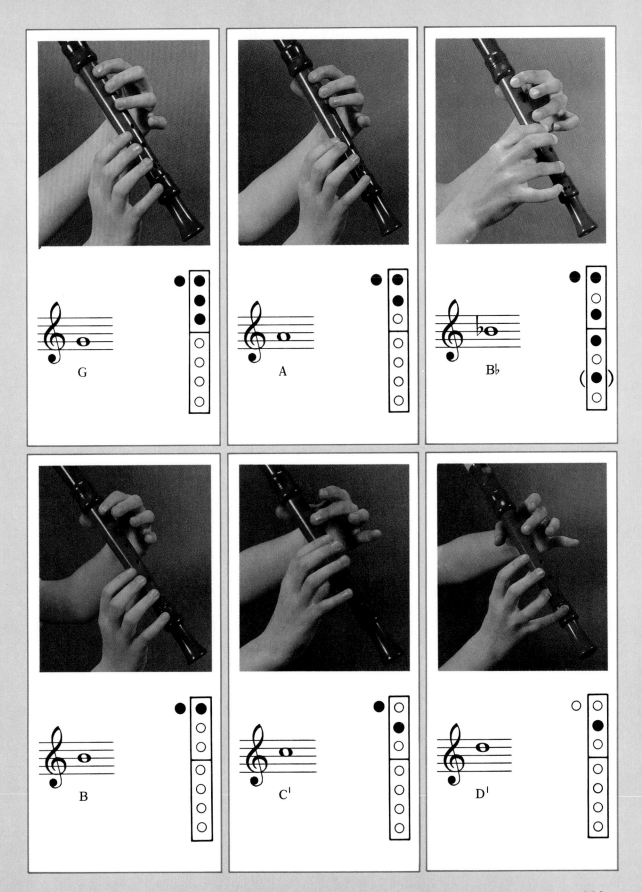

THE MUSICAL MAN

Created by Dorothy Gail Elliott

● Play this musical man. First start at ☆A. Follow the music as many ways as you can.
How many tunes can you play?
Next start at ☆B. How many tunes can you play?

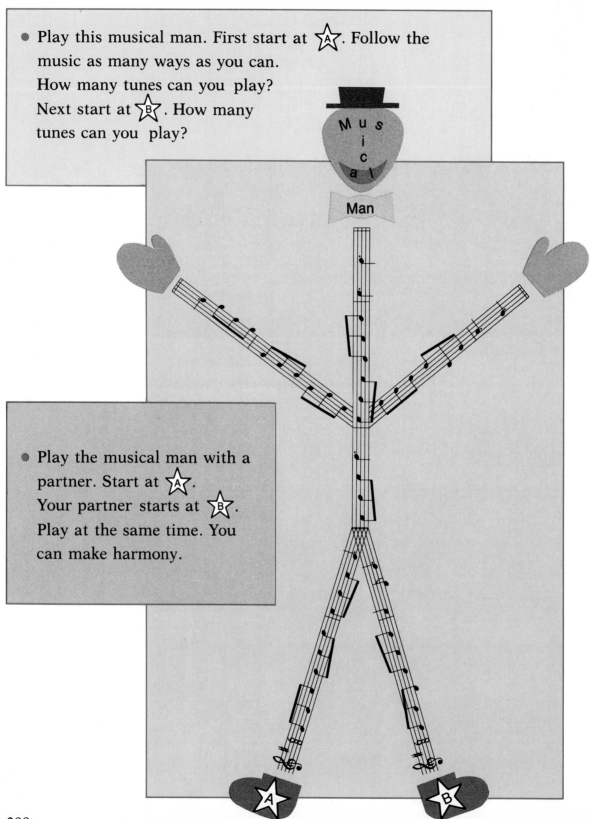

● Play the musical man with a partner. Start at ☆A.
Your partner starts at ☆B.
Play at the same time. You can make harmony.

GLOSSARY OF TERMS

accompaniment musical background for the melody, **200**

al fine sing or play until you reach the word *fine* (the end), **3**

allegro fast, **53**

augmentation lengthening the time-value of notes in a melody, **174**

beat a unit of time, **6**

break strain the brief musical interlude between the trio sections in a march, **167**

call/response song style in which a solo singer takes turns with a group of singers; used by sailors in singing sea chanteys, **13**

canon a musical form that uses imitation; melody played similarly to a round, **103**

capstan chantey song sung by sailors while turning a capstan, a device used to raise and lower the anchor, **14**

cloud chamber bowls a percussion instrument created by Harry Partch using glass jars cut in half and hung so that they vibrate freely, **214**

coda a concluding section of a piece of music, **146**

concert band a group of woodwind, brass, and percussion instruments, **151**

crescendo (<) to gradually get louder, **40**

D.C. (*Da Capo*) to repeat from the beginning, **3**

descant a simple melody, often higher in pitch, that is sung with the main melody, **68**

decrescendo (>) to gradually get softer, **31**

diminuendo to gradually get softer, **31**

dotted quarter note (♩.) sounds as long as three eighth notes, **125**

drum cadence a pattern used to accompany marching, usually sixteen beats long, **166**

dynamics softness or loudness in music, **57**

eighth note (♪) a symbol for a sound in music that is one-eighth as long as the sound of a whole note, **7**

fermata (⌢) a symbol placed over a note to show that it is to be held longer than it normally lasts, **19**

fine the end, **3**

first and second strains in a march, the short, melodically contrasting sections that follow a brief introduction, **167**

flat (♭) symbol indicating that a tone is to be lowered by a half step, **216**

forecastle chantey sailors' song named for the part of the ship where the sailors gathered for the evening; sung for fun and recreation, **15**

forte (f) loud, **57**

fortissimo (ff) very loud, **58**

half note (♩) a symbol for a sound in music that is one-half as long as the sound of a whole note, **43**

harmony the sounding of two or more tones at the same time, **35**

key signature symbol or symbols at the beginning of a piece of music showing what pitches should be sharp or flat throughout the piece, **216**

legato smooth and connected, **45**

lento slow, **53**

long-haul (halyard) chantey song sung by sailors during long jobs, such as hoisting the large sails, **16**

major describes the basic sound of certain songs and scales; songs in major are sometimes described as sounding "happy," **78**

march music having a strongly marked rhythm, **167**

marching band a group of brass, woodwind, and percussion instruments that are played while the performers march, **152**

measure set of notes between two bar lines, **156**

melody the tune of a piece of music, in which high and low pitches sound one after another in rhythm, moving upward, downward, or staying the same, **10**

meter the grouping of beats and accents within a measure, as shown by the meter signature, **66**

meter signature the two numbers on the staff at the beginning of a piece of music that tell how beats are grouped and the kind of note that equals one beat, **208**

mezzo medium, **88**

mezzo forte (mf) medium loud, **88**

mezzo piano (mp) medium soft, **88**

minor the basic sound of certain songs and scales; songs in minor are sometimes described as sounding "sad," **78**

obbligato an accompanying part, **167**

octave the distance of eight steps from one tone to the next tone with the same letter name, **35**

orchestra a large group of instrumental performers, usually including four families of instruments—strings, woodwinds, brass, and percussion, **150**

ostinato a rhythm or melody pattern that keeps repeating throughout a musical piece, **76**

pianissimo (pp) very soft, **58**

piano (p) soft, **57**

pitch how high or low a sound is, **32**

presto very fast, **53**

quarter note (♩) symbol for a sound in music that is one-fourth as long as the sound of a whole note, **7**

quarter rest (𝄽) a symbol for a period of silence that lasts as long as the sound of a quarter note, **18**

ragtime an early style of jazz popular in the 1890s, **105**

refrain a section of a song which repeats at the end of each stanza or verse; sometimes called the chorus, **18**

rhythm the pattern of beats in a piece of music, **43**

rondo a musical form with a repeating main theme, **114**

round song in which the voices sing the same melody but begin at different times, **108**

sea chantey song sung by sailors to help them work together by keeping the beat; also sung for entertainment, **12**

sharp (♯) a symbol indicating that a note is to be raised by a half step, **216**

short haul chanteys songs sung by sailors while pulling ropes when only a few short pulls were needed, **13**

sixteenth note (♬) a symbol for a sound in music that is one-sixteenth as long as the sound of a whole note, **163**

staccato notes having a distinctly separate sound; sometimes marked with dots over or under them, **45**

symphonic band *see* concert band

syncopation rhythm that has sounds or silences where you do not normally expect them, **74**

synthesizer electronic instrument that can imitate the sound of almost any existing instrument, **215**

tempo speed of the beat, **12**

texture the pattern of musical sound formed when different pitches are played or sung together, **108**

theme melody upon which a musical piece is based, **22**

tie (⌣) a curved line that connects two notes of the same pitch and indicates that the sound should be held for the length of both notes, **74**

tonal center the pitch around which the melody of a particular piece seems to center; often the last note of the song, **33**

trio the third part of a march, **167**

unison several people singing or playing a single melody at the same time, **113**

variation a change in rhythm, form, melody, or elements in music that still keeps the original idea of the piece, **10**

verse words and music that make up the body of the song and come before the refrain, **18**

whole note (𝅝) a symbol for a long sound in music, **43**

CLASSIFIED INDEX

Folk and Traditional Songs

Africa
Funga Alafia, **272**

American Indian
Baked Potato, **125**
Loneliness Song, **65**
Paiute Stick Game Song, **62**

Black American
Boatman, The, **245**
Ezekiel Saw the Wheel, **250**
Follow the Drinkin' Gourd, **160**
Go, Tell It on the Mountain, **265**
Great Day, **112**
Trampin', **247**
Who Built the Ark? **172**

British Isles
Girl I Left Behind Me, The, **10**
Twelve Days of Christmas, The, **266**

Canada
Vive la Canadienne, **280**

France
March of the Kings, **86**

Israel
Hava Nashira, **271**
O Hanukah, **76**
Shalom Chaverim, **273**

Jamaica
Mango Walk, **273**

Latin America
Al Citron, **250**

Russia
Troika Song, **116**

United States
Away for Rio, **16**
Banjo Sam, **32**
Billy, Billy, **33**
Blue Tail Fly, **156**
Cape Cod Chantey, **251**
Captain Jinks, **24**
Cindy, **52**
Cotton-Eyed Joe, **269**
Crawdad Hole, **285**
Cumberland Gap, **248**
Cumberland Mountain Bear Chase, **56**
Eight Bells, **270**
Erie Canal, **18**
Fooba Wooba John, **135**
Four in a Boat, **253**
Git Along, Little Dogies, **54**
Going to Boston, **15**
Goober Peas, **144**
Good-Bye, Old Paint, **61**
Great Grand-dad, **59**
Haul Away, Joe, **13**
Hey, Ho! Anybody Home? **271**
Historian, The, **136**
John Kanaka, **246**
Jubilee, **34**
Madalina Catalina, **162**
Nine Hundred Miles, **249**
Old Chisholm Trail, The, **254**
Old Joe Clark, **137**
Page's Train, **248**
Pat Works on the Railroad, **277**
Pay Me My Money Down, **192**
Shenandoah, **14**
Simple Gifts, **20**
Sourwood Mountain, **252**
Sweet Betsy from Pike, **129**
Sun Don't Set in the Morning, **158**
When the Saints Go Marching In, **174**

Holidays and Special Days

December
Breath of Winter, **118**
Carol from an Irish Cabin, **79**
Feliz Navidad, **80**
Fum, Fum, Fum, **263**
Ice and Sleet, **121**
Mama, Bake the Johnny Cake, Christmas Comin', **82**
March of the Kings, **86**
O Hanukah, **76**
Pat-a-Pan, **262**
Twelve Days of Christmas, The, **266**
Winter Fantasy, **75, 92**
Winter's a Drag Rag, **105**
Winter Song, **282**
Winter Thunderstorm Chant, **127**
Winter Wonderland, **264**

Halloween
Boogie Woogie Ghost, The, **46**
Ghost of John, The, **42**

Patriotic
America, the Beautiful, **255**
Battle Hymn of the Republic, **148**
Fifty Nifty United States, **258**
Texas, Our Texas, **275**
This Is My Country, **230**
This Land Is Your Land, **2**
Yankee Doodle, **4**
You're a Grand Old Flag, **256**

Thanksgiving
Come, Ye Thankful People, Come, **66**
For Thy Gracious Blessings, **68**

Musicals
Callin' the Dog
Annie Christmas, **138**
Brown County Fair, The, **132**

Fooba Wooba John, **135**
Historian, The, **136**
Old Joe Clark, **137**
Pecos Bill, **140**

Pioneering
Pioneering, **236**
Spice of America, The, **240**
Unsung Heroes, **238**
Up and Beyond, **242**

Nature, Seasons, Out-of-Doors
Carol from an Irish Cabin, **79**
Come, Ye Thankful People, Come, **66**
Cumberland Gap, **248**
Cumberland Mountain Bear Chase, **56**
Ice and Sleet, **121**
Isn't It Reassuring? **200**
Thank God, I'm a Country Boy, **218**
Troika Song, **116**
Winter Fantasy, **75, 92**
Winter's a Drag Rag, **105**
Winter Song, **282**
Winter Thunderstorm Chant, **127**
Winter Wonderland, **264**

Poems
Buffalo Dusk, **41**
Lightning, **229**
Modern Dragon, A, **38**
Old Christmastide, **89**
Some Opposites, **225**
Ten Tom-Toms, **152**

Travel
Drill, Ye Tarriers, **37**
Page's Train, **248**
Pat Works on the Railroad, **277**
Wabash Cannonball, The, **31**

LISTENING SELECTIONS

Adagio for Glass Harmonica by Wolfgang Amadeus Mozart, **214**

"After You've Gone" by Benny Goodman, **188**

"Battle Hymn" by Morton Gould, **146**

"Bear Dance" by Béla Bartók, **57**

"Cindy," from *Kentucky Mountain Portraits* by Lyndol Mitchell, **53**

"Cloud Chamber Music" by Harry Partch, **214**

"Dances" from *West Side Story* by Leonard Bernstein, **210**

Danse Macabre by Camille Saint-Saëns, **44**

"Farandole," from *L'Arlésienne* by Georges Bizet, **87**

"Festive Overture" by William Grant Still, **161**

"The Girl I Left Behind Me," **9**

"The Girl I Left Behind Me," from *Irish Suite* by Leroy Anderson, **10**

"Grand Walkaround," from *Cakewalk* by Louis Moreau Gottschalk and Hershy Kay, **126**

"Jamaican Rumba" by Arthur Benjamin, **84**

"Leather-Winged Bat," performed by Burl Ives, **146**

"Lightning," with music by Philip Glass, and words by Suzanne Vega, **228**

"On the Sunny Side of the Street," played by the Tommy Dorsey band, **187**

Pacific 231 by Arthur Honegger, **39**

"Peanut Vendor" by Moises S. Rodriguez played by the Stan Kenton band, **209**

"Percussion Variations," from *Young Person's Guide to the Orchestra* by Benjamin Britten, **104**

"Petrushskates" by Joan Tower, **224**

"Pop Corn" by Gershon Kingsley, **215**

"Rondoapplause" by Carl Orff and Gunild Keetman, **115**

"South Rampart Street Parade" by Steve Allen, Ray Bauduc, and Robert Haggart, **176**

"The Stars and Stripes Forever" by John Philip Sousa, **165, 167**

"Street in a Frontier Town," from *Billy the Kid* by Aaron Copland, **97**

"Summertime," from *Porgy and Bess* by George Gershwin (two versions), **189**

🔴 Symphony No. 3 by Roy Harris, **199**

🔴 "Take Five" by Paul Desmond, played by the Dave Brubeck Quartet, **211**

🔴 "Take the A Train," played by Duke Ellington and his band, **188**

🔴 *Toccata*, Third Movement, by Carlos Chávez, **109**

🔴 "Troika," from *Lieutenant Kijé Suite* by Sergei Prokofiev, **117**

🔴 "Variations on Simple Gifts," from *Appalachian Spring* by Aaron Copland, **22**

🔴 "Xylophone Invention" by Carl Orff and Gunild Keetman, **127**

ALPHABETICAL SONG INDEX

A
Al Citron, **250**
Alleluia, **295**
America, the Beautiful, **255**
Annie Christmas, **138**
Away for Rio, **16**

B
Baked Potato, **125**
Banjo Sam, **32**
Battle Hymn of the Republic, **148**
Billy, Billy, **33**
Blue Tail Fly, **156**
Boatman, The, **245**
Boogie Woogie Ghost, The, **46**
Breath of Winter, The, **118**
Brown County Fair, The, **132**

C
Cape Cod Chantey, **251**
Captain Jinks, **24**
Carol from an Irish Cabin, **79**
Carolina in the Morning, **180**
Casey Jones, **268**
Charleston, **178**
Cindy, **52**

Come Follow the Band, **153**
Come, Ye Thankful People, Come, **66**
Cotton-Eyed Joe, **269**
Crawdad Hole, **285**
Cuckoo! **292**
Cumberland Gap, **248**
Cumberland Mountain Bear
    Chase, **56**

D
Ding, Dong, the Bells Do Ring, **103**
Dream of Martin Luther King, The, **110**
Drill, Ye Tarriers, **37**

E
Eight Bells, **270**
Erie Canal, **18**
Ezekiel Saw the Wheel, **250**

F
Feliz Navidad, **80**
Fifty Nifty United States, **258**
Fifth-Ninth Street Bridge Song
    (Feelin' Groovy), **212**
Follow the Drinkin' Gourd, **160**

Fooba Wooba John, **135**
For Thy Gracious Blessings, **68**
Four in a Boat, **253**
Fum, Fum, Fum, **263**
Funga Alafia, **272**

G
Ghost of John, The, **42**
Girl I Left Behind Me, The, **10**
Git Along, Little Dogies, **54**
Going to Boston, **15**
Goober Peas, **144**
Good-Bye, Old Paint, **61**
Go, Tell It on the Mountain, **265**
Great Day, **112**
Great Grand-dad, **59**

H
Harmony, **122**
Haul Away, Joe, **13**
Hava Nashira, **271**
Hey, Ho! Anybody Home? **271**
Historian, The, **136**

I
Ice and Sleet, **121**
Isn't It Reassuring? **200**
It's the Hard-Knock Life, **272**
It's Such a Joy, **190**

J
John Kanaka, **246**
Jubilee, **34**

L
Let There Be Peace on Earth, **90**
Loneliness Song, **65**

M
Macnamara's Band, **182**

Madalina Catalina, **162**
Mama, Bake the Johnny Cake, Christmas
    Comin', **82**
Mango Walk, **273**
March of the Kings, **86**
Midnight, **290**
Mrs. Murphy's Chowder, **185**

N
Nine Hundred Miles, **249**

O
O Hanukah, **76**
Old Chisholm Trail, The, **254**
Old Joe Clark, **137**
On the Sunny Side of the Street, **186**

P
Page's Train, **248**
Paiute Stick Game Song, **62**
Pat-a-Pan, **262**
Pat Works on the Railroad, **277**
Pay Me My Money Down, **192**
Peanut Vendor, **206**
Pecos Bill, **140**
Pioneering, **236**

R
Reach Out and Touch (Somebody's
    Hand), **226**

S
Shalom Chaverim, **273**
Shenandoah, **14**
Simple Gifts, **20**
Skin and Bones, **262**
Snowbird, **274**
Sourwood Mountain, **252**
Spice of America, The, **240**
State Rondo, **114**

Sun Don't Set in the Morning, **158**
Sweet Betsy from Pike, **129**

T
Talking Dust Bowl, **278**
Texas, Our Texas, **275**
Thank God, I'm a Country Boy, **218**
This Is My Country, **230**
This Land Is Your Land, **2**
Tiger Rag, **177**
Tomorrow, **235**
Trampin', **247**
Troika Song, **116**
Twelve Days of Christmas, The, **266**

U
Unsung Heroes, **238**
Up and Beyond, **242**

V
Vine and Fig Tree, **279**
Vive la Canadienne, **280**

W
Wabash Cannonball, The, **31**
We Go Together, **221**
We Watch TV, **281**
When the Saints Go Marching In, **174**
Who Built the Ark? **172**
Winter Fantasy, **75, 92**
Winter's a Drag Rag, **105**
Winter Song, **282**
Winter Thunderstorm Chant, **127**
Winter Wonderland, **264**

Y
Yankee Doodle, **4**
You're a Grand Old Flag, **256**